The Voice of Pope Francis

The Voice of Pope Francis

Communicating to Understand
and Embrace the Other

DARIO EDOARDO VIGANÒ

Translated from the Italian by
Robert H. Hopcke

A Crossroad Book
The Crossroad Publishing Company
New York

THE POPE FRANCIS RESOURCE LIBRARY

The Crossroad Publishing Company
www.CrossroadPublishing.com

English translation copyright 2017
by The Crossroad Publishing Company
A Herder&Herder Book
The Crossroad Publishing Company, New York

Originally published in Italian as *Fratelli e sorelle, buonasera. Papa Francesco e la comunicazione.* ©2016 by Carocci editore, Roma.

Photo credits are on page 186.

The stylized crossed letter C logo is a registered trademark of The Crossroad Publishing Company.

ISBN 978-0-8245-2332-9 (alk. paper)

Library of Congress Cataloging-in-Publication Data available from the Library of Congress.

Cover design by George Foster
Book design by The HK Scriptorium, Inc.

In continuation of our 200-year tradition of independent publishing, The Crossroad Publishing Company proudly offers a variety of books with strong, original voices and diverse perspectives. The viewpoints expressed in our books are not necessarily those of The Crossroad Publishing Company, any of its imprints or of its employees. No claims are made or responsibility assumed for any health or other benefit.

Books published by The Crossroad Publishing Company may be purchased at special quantity discount rates for classes and institutional use. For information, please e-mail sales@CrossroadPublishing.com.

Printed in the United States of America in 2018

Contents

INTRODUCTION

Communicating the Truth

In the space of ten months, Pope Francis has turned around the style of papal communication. He wants speed, spontaneity, sincerity, and conviction. His communication is global. Pope Francis speaks to everyone. He has no preferences because everyone needs his word, which transforms into a message. Francis doesn't like intermediaries in communication. He himself becomes communication with his gestures, spontaneity, and promptness. His message is universal, and it is addressed above all to the existential peripheries of the world. His national and international visits (Lampedusa, Rio de Janeiro, Cagliari, Assisi) illustrate this communicative force, which is more extraordinary than ordinary. For this reason, it is our honor to award him this prize, on behalf of all those who believe in communication that becomes dialogue, conversation, justice, the announcement of fraternity.[1]

With these words, on December 13, 2013, Gino Falleri and Carlo Felice Corsetti, creators of the Argil: European

Man, the international prize for journalism, gave special acknowledgment to Pope Francis, characterizing him as "a person of worldwide prominence, a great global communicator." And that was not the only special honor bestowed on him in those days. Just before that, *Time* magazine named him 2013 "Man of the Year" and featured the new pope of the Catholic Church on its cover, saying, "he took the name of a humble saint and then called for a church of healing. The first non-European pope in 1,200 years is poised to transform a place that measures change by the century,"[2] and *Time*'s managing editor, Nancy Gibbs, in her own editorial piece, summed up the Holy Father's effect. "And yet in less than a year, he has done something remarkable: he has not changed the words, but he's changed the music."[3]

And this recognition came before what was to be a series of very emotional moments that took place, one after another, during his subsequent apostolic visits to the Holy Land and to Turkey (in May and November 2014), to Sarajevo, South America, Cuba, and the United States of America (in June, July, and September 2015), followed by travel to Africa for the opening of the Holy Door (in November 2015) and then on to Mexico (in February 2016) with a stop in Cuba, where he held a historic meeting with Patriarch Kirill of Moscow, among all the many other public appearances during his first years in which Jorge Mario Bergoglio put himself forward to engage the world. But, here, only nine months after his election, both of these acknowledgments were confirmation of the unusual enthusiasm that his person inspired in the media, among believers and nonbelievers alike.

Right from his very first public appearance on the evening of March 13, 2013, Bergoglio was seen as a pope who could profoundly transform the Church's way of communicating. Even before he even stepped out on that balcony over St. Peter's Square, Cardinal Protodeacon Jean-Louis Tauran's announcement of his election spurred journalists and commentators the world over to begin asking on live television what the selection of his name would and could mean, in that this was the first time in history a pope had taken the name of the Holy Man of Assisi, that lover of poverty, he who had chosen to live with the least fortunate, the most lowly. Francis is a name that immediately suggests humility but also, of course, in a certain way, a revolutionary spirit, someone with the will to truly change things.

In the days that followed, nearly every journalist, in countless articles and features that appeared in the newspapers, television, radio, and online, went on to list even more signs of changes to come. Looking through a "political" lens, they pointed out that this was the first pope to come from South America, not just the first non-European, and moreover that the numerous papal prognostications that had been bandied about prior to the opening of the conclave hadn't even brought up the name of this bishop from Buenos Aires who was well known in Argentina, true, and yet all but unknown anywhere else.

Much would be also made of what any number of his initial actions seemed to symbolize, for example, his preference for basic liturgical vestments and a simple, sober style of dressing, which was interpreted as his distancing himself from previous forms and fashions of papal royalty. With the passage of months, and then years, however, it became ever more obvious that Pope Francis was engaged in a more substantial project, namely, revolutionizing communication in ways intended to renew dialogue with the larger world, continuing in the spirit initially set forth in the "Pastoral Constitution on the Church in the Modern World," *Gaudium et spes,* and that Francis would be doing this by directly addressing some of the most fundamental questions facing society today.

In these first few years of his pontificate, we have all had an opportunity to get to know Bergoglio better and to witness his particular gift at establishing relationships, his innate knack for reaching out in a neighborly way, his capacity to create rapport and overcome the distance between people. His capacity for relationship is what makes all his words and deeds comprehensible to everyone, to believers as well as nonbelievers. As semiologist Algirdas Julien Greimas would say, in the way that Pope Francis goes about framing what he has to say, there are no opponents.[4]

His style of communication, which, like the Gospels, eludes easy categorization, is thus difficult to pin down across the vast media panorama of the modern world. One hint concerning his communication style and its intentions comes from Bergoglio himself, in his own words, when he says, perhaps somewhat surprisingly:

How, then, can communication be at the service of an authentic culture of encounter? What does it mean for us, as disciples of the Lord, to encounter others in the light of the Gospel? In spite of our own limitations and sinfulness, how do we draw truly close to one another? These questions are summed up in what a scribe—a communicator—once asked Jesus: "And who is my neighbor?" (Luke 10:29). This question can help us to see communication in terms of "neighborliness." We might paraphrase the question in this way: How can we be "neighborly" in our use of the communications media and in the new environment created by digital technology? I find an answer in the parable of the Good Samaritan, which is also a parable about communication. Those who communicate, in effect, become neighbors. The Good Samaritan not only draws nearer to the man he finds half-dead on the side of the road; he takes responsibility for him. Jesus shifts our understanding: it is not just about seeing the other as someone like myself, but of the ability to make myself like the other. Communication is really about realizing that we are all human beings, children of God. I like seeing this power of communication as "neighborliness."[5]

This is communication, not as a form of manipulation, the pope insists, but rather as understanding, as the embrace of another, so as to overcome the stumbling blocks of diversity and the sharp blades of exclusivity. Revolutionary as this message may seem at first blush, it is nevertheless derived directly from the Gospels and from the teachings of Jesus. So, when Bergoglio uses the figure of the Good Samaritan from the parable, whose name has become synonymous with a spirit of selfless generosity, to illustrate his ideal of communication, it is not mere happenstance. As we will see, in his world, the word that saves, the word that "sees" the other, that goes forth to meet the other in dialogue, the word that incarnates the supreme gift of mercy, that word is the form of communication Pope Francis tirelessly promotes and practices, an authentically "catholic" word that leaves no one behind and excludes no one from the conversation.

Because of his way of communicating, Francis quickly became one of the most beloved of popes, listened to and quoted by believers and nonbelievers alike. But it would be a mistake to think that all of the above are the result of implementing some sort of facile, superficial, or banal "communication strategy" on his part. Quite the opposite: this pope's communications touch everyone because, with the great awareness and sophistication of his cultural and linguistic resources, he succeeds in approaching the impossible "degree zero" that semiologist Roland Barthes wrote about, when in writing, all defects are corrected, resulting in a true mythology born from the language of literature.[6] This "degree zero" is, ultimately, impossible, says Barthes, because there is no writing (as a social manifestation of language) that is not compromised in some way by that which he calls "power," by a dominant culture that excludes and marginalizes. Impossible, declares Barthes—and yet Pope Francis's communications come very close to reaching this "degree zero": imposed by no one, understood by all.

In the pages to come, we will be examining the range of symbolic pathways that his way of communicating follows, analyzing various aspects of this papacy's "public image," starting with his initial greeting that night on a very crowded St. Peter's Square and onward, through his apostolic visitations, in both his homilies and his encyclicals, so as to broaden our perspective and articulate ever more clearly the ways in which his message, as read on a variety of levels, succeeds in the end to come—and touch—us all.

ONE

Francis, Plain and Simple

I don't go around carrying the keys to an atomic bomb in my bag. Please! I carry my bag because that's what I've always done. When I travel, I bring it with me. What's inside? Well, I have my razor, my breviary, my calendar; I bring a book to read. This time I brought along one of St. Therese's writings because I have a devotion to her. I've always carried a bag with me when I travel; it's just the normal thing to do. We should all be normal. I don't know, I think it's strange that that photo has been seen now around the world. We really should get used to being normal, living our lives in a normal way.[1]

A Transformative Ceremony

"Brothers and sisters, good evening!" In that moment, the whole world stopped and then found itself moved by the new pope's first greeting from the Balcony of Blessing in St. Peter's, March 13, 2013. Just as engaging was the tone of the words that followed. "You know that it was the duty of the conclave to give Rome a bishop. It seems that my brother cardinals have gone to the ends of the earth to get one . . . but here we are. . . . I thank you for your welcome." In a scene that has since become engraved in our collective memory, these first few words of the newly elected pontiff bring to mind immediately equally memorable words spoken in the same circumstances, on live television, thirty-five years earlier by Karol Wojtyła,[2] another pope "from far away" and likewise gifted as a communicator.[3]

That live television played a part in both events is not a minor detail and should not be overlooked. Most certainly at the time of John Paul II's election and for a large part of the world's people at the time of Francis's, television was the primary way to experience the happenings in St. Peter's Square. Thus, through the medium of television, what occurs becomes an event that, in turn, becomes itself a form of communication.

After his greeting to the crowd, the new pope delivered his first, brief address, praying for his predecessor, Pope Emeritus Benedict XVI, and extending the hope that all might proceed forward in brotherhood. But before imparting his traditional first blessing, he did something that surprised all the faithful, both those in the square and those watching on TV, and which caught those in the media off guard. He opened his arms and turned to the people celebrating below: "And now I would like to give the blessing, but first, first I ask a favor of you: before the bishop blesses his people, I ask you to pray to the Lord that he will bless me: the prayer of the people asking the blessing for their bishop. Let us make, in silence, this prayer: your prayer over me."

And with these words, the noisy crowd grew quiet and joined the pontiff in prayer, as he folded his hands and bowed his head: for the twenty interminable seconds that follow, the television screens of the entire world had no choice but to train themselves on the very powerful scene of the motionless crowd there, a tide of humanity holding its breath, immersed in a vibrantly charged, heartfelt silence. Such a weighty silence, so alien to the ways of television, was probably the most important moment of his entire first address, as Aldo Grasso would emphasize in his article in *Corriere della Sera*:

> Let us say right off that the most spiritual act, unexpected and in many ways quite upsetting, was the moment of welcome, those long moments of silence in which the new pope asked the faithful in the square for their intercession by way of a sacred blessing: "I ask you to pray God to bless your bishop." That silence was worth more than all the words: a pontificate that begins with such an intense and uproarious silence (in the absence of uproar) announces that something new will be coming from here on. And in the days since, these images have remained charged with an extraordinary symbolic value.... His first words have now been repeated endlessly: "It seems that my brother cardinals have gone to the ends of the earth to get a pope . . . but here we are...."

Twenty minutes later, the announcement of the new papacy was tweeted by @Pontifex, the account that had been suspended on the day that Benedict XVI stepped down: "Habemus Papam Franciscum."[4]

We stand before a "transformative" ceremony here, a turning point,

> A liminal moment of the ceremony itself—the moment of interruption of routinized social time— stops history in its tracks. It invites society to consider alternative routes and, in doing so, to re-experience some of the chaos, anguish, and exhilaration of its genesis. New projects are born, in the light of which the past is reinvented and collected memory is reorganized.[5]

I believe that every one of us, right from the start of Bergoglio's ministry, has had the distinct impression that this pope was putting himself forward as a missionary on behalf of the Church, ready to go to the ends of the earth as a witness to Jesus Christ and to carry the Gospel of mercy to all people. His heartfelt words inspire children, grown-ups, believers, and nonbelievers, all of whom wish to meet him at least once in their lives. The strength of Pope Francis lies in the feeling that arises from an encounter with the man, an encounter that is always and in every way warmly fraternal, out of his lived conviction that solidarity and closeness come from the relationships between individuals throughout the human family. This family of humanity is seen by him as one, with both rights and also obligations to the world around us, and in it we all assume the responsibility of a global citizenship for the well-being of future generations. Francis reinforces this essential view by way of his subsequent encyclical *Laudato si'*, and continues his struggle—a struggle he shared fully even with those from cultures quite distant from his—for the future of the entire planet.

But, to go back for a moment to appreciate the natural intuitiveness of Pope Francis's ability to communicate, by opening the whole conversation with that "good evening," itself signaling his intention to speak "on two levels" at once—self-conscious and yet also fully in the moment— he creates a feeling of sharing among those listening, an experience of community in the Church and the world that is confirmed by his words.

In the first moments when that man who would soon become known as the "People's Pope" met the world, he spoke to satisfy a need: the Church, which has been tested by many difficulties and scandals of recent history, was being put on notice that from now on, familiarity and simplicity would be the order of the day. By taking this approach, of course, Francis revealed a great deal about his personality and his way of communicating: his sober style, his humility, the way he relishes conversation and direct contact, which would be on display in all his public appearances, particularly in his fondness for hugging.[6] Later on, as his papacy continued, we would also begin to hear a more decisive tone creep into his voice, a steady assertiveness, but that evening, in those brief moments on the balcony over St. Peter's Square, we were able to glimpse certain traits of Francis's personality that would from that time forward remain unchanged in the collective imagination: his accessibility, his pragmatism, his transparency, his warmth and common touch. In a word, his humanity.

An event of historic proportions such as the election of the pope cannot help but change the world, and Francis's public image on television, a media event in its own right, is destined to produce in its own way changes not just in public opinion but in people's behavior, in the social geography of the world, so to speak, as well as changes over the long term in both the agendas and direction of our political institutions. We can thus say that from that evening on, the world was changed and was changed by way of words and images.

> Such festive viewing leads to that alternative model of social life in which the usual down-to-earth, "indicative" approach to social reality gives way to a "subjunctive" *and utopian openness to alternative possibilities.*[7]

Thus, communication, especially on the sort of global stage that the papacy offers, is not mere form: it becomes substance. For this reason, communication must be explored as a basic part of the pastoral ministry of Pope Francis. However, our inquiry into rhetorical and communicative structures that are his and his alone and that give rise to interventions as textually complex as the encyclicals, nevertheless starts from a far-off place. Just where did this pope come from, he and his inimitable style that would profoundly change the Church?

"The Lord was waiting for me,
having chosen me in his mercy."

The first of five children, Jorge Mario Bergoglio was born in Buenos Aires on December 17, 1936, to parents of Italian descent. His father, Mario José, was from Piedmont and had come to Argentina in 1928 to join other relatives who had started a small local business there, and he found employment with the railroad. During that time, he met Regina Maria Sivori, herself likewise an immigrant, from Liguria. After the birth of the future pope, they would go on to have four more children, Oscar Adrian in 1938, Marta Regina in 1940, Alberto Horacio in 1942, and Maria Elena in 1948.

Mario José did not leave Italy by himself, however. An only child, he brought his mother, Rosa, with him, both devout Catholics who had, before emigrating, been active in the newly founded *Azione cattolica di San Martino di Asti* and whose teachings the young Jorge Mario would always keep before him as a source of inspiration. When he felt a vocation to religious life, the first person with whom he shared his desire was his father: "He reacted well. In fact, he said he was happy about it. I was sure my father would understand. His mother had been an extremely pious person, and from her he inherited both her devotion and her strength, the two of them united in the sorrow they felt for having left their homeland."[8]

Nonna Rosa became, in a way, one of the most important relationships during Bergoglio's childhood, alongside that of his mother, Regina: therefore, that the pope reflects frequently on the importance of women and female role models in the life of the family is not by chance:

> At the center of the Church's life is the Mother of Jesus. Perhaps mothers, so ready to sacrifice themselves for their own children and, not infrequently, for the children of others as well, need to be listened to more. We would do well to understand their daily struggle to be good at their work and to be attentive and loving within their families; we would do well to understand better what they aspire to, how they wish to express the best and most authentic fruits of their liberation. A woman with children always has problems, always has work before her. I remember in the home where I grew up, there were five of us, one here, one there, with my poor mother running back and forth all the time. But she was happy. She gave us all so much.[9]

In this way, Bergoglio's simplicity is not, nor does it come off as, simply rhetorical in style, because it arises from real experience, growing up within a big family in humble circumstances. Around the age of eighteen, an event occurred that was destined to change the course of his life.

On September 21, 1954, I was thrown from a horse. I knew P. Carlos B. Duarte Ibarra from Flores (my parish), so I made my confession to him, just in case . . . and there—though I wasn't sitting in a tax booth like Matthew, whose feast day it was that day—the Lord came to me, "choosing me in his mercy." From that point on, I have never had any doubts about being a priest.[10]

Miserando atque eligendo becomes the motto that he chose when elected bishop and that he would use for the papal coat of arms, perhaps because it makes reference to the merciful, salvific love of God that Francis never tires of recalling, perhaps in remembrance of that day in 1954, on the Feast of St. Matthew,[11] in which he felt the call:

That is the moment in which I bumped into God's mercy, and so I used this as my episcopal motto: September 21 is the feast day of St. Matthew, and the Venerable Bede, discussing the conversion of Matthew, says that Jesus saw Matthew *miserando atque eligendo*. It's an expression impossible to translate, because in Italian and in Spanish, neither of the gerunds has a subject. The literal translation would be something like "pitying and choosing," a bit like a work of manual labor. "He had mercy on him": that's the literal translation of the text. Years later, during a recitation of my Latin breviary, I came upon this passage, and I realized that the Lord had worked on me to shape me in his mercy. Every time I went to Rome,

I would go to the Church of San Luigi dei Francesi to pray before Caravaggio's painting *The Calling of Saint Matthew.*[12]

In keeping with how he began, Jorge Mario Bergoglio quickly adopts an attitude of openness and dialogue: he listens for the mystery of God but also seeks out whoever can help him move forward.[13] He speaks of this himself in a long letter from 1990 that he wrote to the Argentinean Church historian Cayetano Bruno, in which he recalls his younger days, and in particular Enrique Pozzoli, the Salesian father from Italy who had baptized him (on Christmas Day 1936) and who served as his first important spiritual guide:

> I felt my call to the priesthood for the first time at Ramos Mejía, during the sixth grade, and I spoke of it to our well-known "fisher" of vocation, Father Martinez, SDB. But then, I began high school and so, "see you later!" I studied chemistry at the industrial/technical high school and I used to spend a lot of time (especially during the summer) in my maternal grandparents' house on Calle Quinto Bocayuno. . . . I spoke no more about it at home until November 1955: that was the year I graduated from Industrial (a six-year program) and enrolled in chemical engineering studies. At home, they remained dubious. They were devout, practicing Catholics. . . . But they did think it best that I wait a few years, continue my studies at the university. Since I realized eventually

upon whom the resolution of the question actually rested, I took myself to Father Pozzoli and told him everything. He explored the discernment of my vocation with me, and told me to pray and to put everything in God's hands.[14]

It was thanks to Fr. Pozzoli and his exhortation to trust in God's will that the young Jorge Mario came to choose the priesthood after a time: he graduated with a degree in chemistry from the University of Buenos Aires and afterward continued to work and spend time with friends. However, the notion of dedicating his life, ultimately, to the Church was never far from his mind even then, and eventually his family decided themselves to consult with Fr. Pozzoli. Continuing in his letter to Cayetano Bruno, he tells how decisive the priest's intervention in the matter was and how the conversation, in the end, became a genuine Socratic dialogue of sorts:

> What freedom of spirit is required to discern one's vocation! Halfway through breakfast, the question was raised. Fr. Pozzoli says that university studies are going well, but that one takes up tasks at the time God wishes one to take them up, and begins to tell various stories of how people came to their vocations (without taking sides), ending with the story of his own. Naturally, Fr. Pozzoli didn't end by telling my parents to send me to seminary nor by even expecting a decision from them.... Rather, we realized that it was a matter of "softening them up," which

he helped with, after which what would be would be.
That was typical of him: *una de cal y otra de arena* (a
little lime, a little sand, or as we say it, the carrot-and-
stick approach). One might not know where one was
headed . . . but he did: and generally he didn't want
to get there ahead of you so that it appeared he had
"won." When he "sniffed around" to see if he could
get what he wanted, he'd often then pull way back
before one even noticed he had. So the decision was
made on one's own, freely, on the part of whomever
he was speaking with. One never felt forced, and yet,
he had prepared one's heart for it. He had planted the
seed and planted it well, but he let others enjoy reap-
ing the harvest.[15]

The dialectic modality used by Fr. Pozzoli puts one in
mind, clever as it was, with no disrespect intended by that
phrase, with the ways of a particular Jesuit: Ignatius of
Loyola, in fact, and his principle of *"entra con la suya para
salir con la nuestra,"*[16] which indicates how to encounter
and dialogue with another, for to convince someone of
something, one must first enter fully into his or her way
of thinking. As Bergoglio would put it, once he was pope,
"truth is an encounter,"[17] and so, having been raised in the
faith under the aegis of a man like Fr. Pozzoli, it is no surprise that Jorge Mario would in the end choose to become
a member of the Society of Jesus.

Having made his decision and supported by his whole
family, Jorge Mario entered the seminary of Villa Devoto

in 1956. The following summer he contracted pneumonia, with some serious complications, such that surgery was necessary to save his life, followed by a long period of convalescence, during which Fr. Pozzoli's visits were of great comfort. Once recovered, Bergoglio did not return to the seminary, however. In 1958, he instead joined the Jesuits, spending his novitiate studying philosophy and theology in Chile. Once back in Buenos Aires, he received his degree in both those areas of study. Eleven year later, on December 13, 1969, he was ordained a priest.

Thanks to his charismatic personality, he was named Father Provincial of Argentina at the age of only thirty-six and remained in the leadership of the Society there in South America until 1980, when he took the position of rector at the college where he had studied, San Miguel. For a dozen years or so, he pursued his studies and taught philosophy, theology, psychology, and literature, until 1992, when John Paul II named him auxiliary bishop of Buenos Aires, and then archbishop in 1998.

There would be fifteen years more before he was elected to the pontificate, a time during which Bergoglio invested the majority of his time in ministry within his diocese, which he came to call "la mi Esposa"—my Wife—and which he considered his true mission. He kept a low profile, spent time among the people, used public transportation to cover the many kilometers required for him to reach the outskirts of the diocese. Indeed, "outskirts" would be one of the key words in his discourse to the General Congregation on March 9, 2013: "The Church is called to go out from itself and to go to the outskirts, not just geographical outskirts, but the outskirts of existential experience: the margins of the mysteries of sin, pain, injustice, ignorance, religious indifference, of thought, of any form of suffering," he would say to the cardinals who had come together for the conclave, inviting them to elect a pope capable of taking the Church in that direction, out of the bubble of self-referentiality into which it had enclosed itself, "making itself sick."

In the end, it was he whom they elected, a man whose primary concern for many years had been how to carry the presence of the Church into places within his diocese that had been abandoned by the government. For this reason, during his time as bishop, Bergoglio vigorously promoted pastoral activity on all levels, exhorting his priests to turn their parishes into the living heart of their communities, building new churches, and, where possible, even designating garages and private homes as places of prayer and worship, available to one and all: what was important was to build a network of presence, by way of his so-called "600-meter strategy," a notion that came to him after reading a sociology study that showed this distance was the range of influence a single parish had on the surrounding neighborhood.

Meanwhile, in 2001, John Paul II made him a cardinal, and four years later, at the 2005 conclave that would elect Joseph Ratzinger, Bergoglio garnered a fair number of votes, though he was still relatively unknown to most people. That year he was elected president of the Argentine

Episcopal Conference, which in 2007 would have a major impact in Brazil, at the 5th Annual General Conference of Latin-American Bishops meeting at the National Shrine of Our Lady of Aparecida. The document produced by this conference presents a Church infused with great vitality, poised for action, "on a mission," as Bergoglio would put it, such that on February 23, 2013, Pope Benedict XVI—a mere five days before his resignation became effective—named him a member of the Pontifical Commission for Latin America.

Ratzinger himself has often remarked on the humility and spirit of service his successor embodies, not to mention how, even as a cardinal, Bergoglio remained distinctly disengaged from any sort of "ecclesiastical careerism" and indeed explicitly declared himself in opposition to the "spiritual worldliness" he saw afflicting the clergy.[18] In an interview published at the time of the March 2012 consistory, he said:

> To be a cardinal is a service, not an honorific to brag about. Vanity, bragging about oneself, is an attitude of spiritual worldliness which is the worst sin in the Church. The error of this way of thinking is mentioned in the final pages of Henri du Lubac's *Meditation on the Church*. Spiritual worldliness is a religious anthropocentrism that has Gnostic aspects to it. Careerism, seeking always to advance oneself, is a big part of this sort of spiritual worldliness. As is often said about the reality of vainglory: look at the

peacock, how beautiful when seen from the front, but take a couple more steps and look at it from the back, and there you see the ugly reality. Whoever gives oneself over to such solipsistic vanity suffers greatly deep inside.[19]

In 2014, Bergoglio, now pope, before the Roman Curia, listed various "curial diseases" among which was

the disease of idolizing superiors. This is the disease of those who court their superiors in the hope of gaining their favor. They are victims of careerism and opportunism; they honor persons and not God (cf. Matt 23:8-12). They serve thinking only of what they can get and not of what they should give. Smallminded persons, unhappy and inspired only by their own lethal selfishness (cf. Gal 5:16-25). Superiors themselves could be affected by this disease, when they court their collaborators in order to obtain their submission, loyalty, and psychological dependency, but the end result is a real complicity.[20]

Bergoglio has long held the strong conviction that service always brings with it a dimension of humility, a setting aside of oneself so as to have direct contact with the reality of life and other people. When, for example, in 2001, he was offered a curial position of considerable importance, he firmly refused it with a simple, direct statement: "Please. I would die in the Curia."

Once elected pope, his need for contact with others, his need to be physically close, would remain strong within him, and he would live in the same simple, quiet way that made him so beloved among the Argentineans during his time as bishop in Buenos Aires; and though some seemed shocked at his decision to continue to live at Casa di Santa Marta, he defended his choice as only natural. In a letter dated May 15, 2013, to his life-long friend Fr. Enrique Martinez, pastor of the Church of the Annunciation in Buenos Aires, he wrote: "I didn't want to go live in the Apostolic Palace. I only go there to work and for audiences ... which does me a bit of good and keeps me from isolating myself."[21]

And again, in an unequivocal way, he makes the same point during a May 2015 interview in the Argentine magazine *La Voz del Pueblo*:

> Psychologically, I cannot survive without other people around me. I'm not a monk. That is why I stayed here [at Santa Marta]. This is a guest house, there are some 120 rooms, and about forty of us who work for the Holy See are in residence here, while the rest are guests: bishops, priests, laypeople who are passing through and whom we host here. This is a good thing. To come here, to eat in the dining room where everyone comes together, to celebrate Mass where four times a week there are visitors, from various parishes ... I really like it. I became a priest to be with people. I thank God that I've never lost this desire to be with others.[22]

The effective, sincere expression of such a simplicity of spirit brings forth a response equally simple and spontaneous: in every encounter, many people press forward to engage in the conversation that Bergoglio invites with every one of his public appearances or addresses.[23] His audiences began to draw so many of the faithful that it became impossible to continue to hold them in the Paul VI Audience Hall, such that the traditional weekly event would come to be held in St. Peter's Square, where at times there have been an estimated 70,000 people in attendance. Even on these occasions, Pope Francis shows himself sensitive to the needs of those present: for those affected by the weather—infants, the elderly, the infirm—he will see them first inside the audience hall, and then only afterward proceed outside, for the rest of the time. The same happens during his apostolic visitations: at every stop, huge crowds gather to celebrate his coming, and the Holy Father will ask to stop the Popemobile so he can get out, touch, hug, and kiss the neediest among the crowd countless times throughout the event, yet another reason Jorge Mario Bergoglio will be called, from the start, "the People's Pope." In public, he comes across as someone who knows where he came from and who lives in accordance with the values of simplicity, clarity, humility, and generosity learned from the family he grew up in and from long experience throughout his life as a priest and pastor.

What shaped his formation as a priest is of particular interest to us because it will be given voice in one of his most significant writings, his apostolic exhortation

Evangelii gaudium, which he alone signed[24] and in which he addresses the challenge of proclaiming the Gospel to today's world. We will examine what he says in this document more fully in Chapter 3, but first we must appreciate the symbolic roots of his pontificate in the persons of two saints—Francis of Assisi and Ignatius of Loyola—each quite different from the other but both of whom leave their indelible stamp on Pope Francis's notion of communication as conversation and as "linguistic action."

The Legacy of the Holy Man of Assisi

Bergoglio is the first Jesuit to be chosen for the papal chair, and he is the first to choose the name Francis. So, let us here take the time to appreciate the symbolic value of the name he took and the implications of his decision.

To choose to carry the name of Assisi's saint was intended to communicate something important, and Bergoglio himself explained his reasons for his choice in an audience with representatives of the communications media a few days after his election:

> Some people wanted to know why the Bishop of Rome wished to be called Francis. Some thought of Francis Xavier, Francis de Sales, and also Francis of Assisi. I will tell you the story. During the election, I was seated next to the Archbishop Emeritus of São Paolo and Prefect Emeritus of the Congregation for the Clergy, Cardinal Claudio Hummes: a good friend, a good friend! When things were looking

dangerous, he encouraged me. And when the votes reached two-thirds, there was the usual applause, because the pope had been elected. And he gave me a hug and a kiss, and said: "Don't forget the poor!" And those words came to me: the poor, the poor. Then, right away, thinking of the poor, I thought of Francis of Assisi. Then I thought of all the wars, as the votes were still being counted, till the end. Francis is also the man of peace. That is how the name came into my heart: Francis of Assisi. For me, he is the man of poverty, the man of peace, the man who loves and protects creation; these days we do not have a very good relationship with creation, He is the man who gives us this spirit of peace, a poor man. . . . Ah, how much I would love a poor Church and a church for the poor.[25]

Poverty, peace, protector of creation—all will be themes emphasized throughout Bergoglio's pontificate; and though one cannot really go so far as to characterize this address to the media in one of his first audiences as a "plan" for his papacy, in the end, that is what it becomes. Through the choice of this name, in fact, Bergoglio expressly declares that he will take to himself the legacy of Assisi's saint, abide by his teachings, and follow his interpretation of the Gospel as exemplary. Francis of Assisi, indeed,

> is the saint who communes with all creatures in the universe, but who is also the saint of poverty, brotherhood, and love for one's neighbor, the saint who

is united in passionate union with Jesus Christ and who embraces suffering as a gift from God. All of these are aspects of the beauty of Francis's image. What this pope has done is to redeem all of these aspects, leaving none of them behind.[26]

But Francis is not just the patron saint of the poor; he is a profoundly dialectic figure, both in how he breaks with tradition, fearlessly challenging the rules and assumptions of his time with disruptive acts on both practical and symbolic levels, but also in the gentler and more reassuring sense of how he represents a religious tradition that engages in dialogue with all creatures, from the smallest to the greatest and most ferocious.

Among the first persons to underscore the similarities between the new pope and the holy man of Assisi with regard to their approach to people was Nobel Laureate in Literature Dario Fo, anticlerical to his roots and yet intrigued by the figure Bergoglio presented: "I listened to him with full attention. There was no pretense. All he said came from clean, pure, conscious thinking, such that what he said was valuable, stayed in one's memory, got people's attention."[27] In the TV program *Francis: Lu Santo Jullare,* which aired on RAI July 22, 2014, Fo rewrote the text of his theater piece from 1999 that dealt with the saint from Assisi, updating it and adding into the dialogue various words from the new pontiff. One trait embodied by St. Francis that immediately calls to mind the figure of the Argentine pope is that "he inveighs heavily against those members of the Church who have fallen victim to their desire to enjoy their lives here on earth without giving thought to Heaven; he takes action against spiritual laxity and the thirst for money."[28]

Moreover, St. Francis is an itinerant pilgrim, a man who chose to live in the streets and to immerse himself in the realities of this world, who preaches in the town square and who engages the people around him in their own native Umbrian dialect, despite his own more sophisticated, middle-class education and upbringing. In the same way, Bergoglio goes about his day, and, despite his erudite theological training, he prefers in public situations to adopt a simple, accessible way of talking—a pope who, when all is said and done, loves the company of people, who craves direct contact and dialogue, who enjoys being engaged in a relationship of speaking and listening, a pope in the middle of things but who never puts himself center-stage.

Listening is a necessary part of the communication process, in which silence is the first requirement, an indispensable condition for receiving what is said and what it means. Consequently, the more one is comfortable remaining silent, the more valuable will be the words one offers when one speaks, the eventual fruit of one's inward meditation. Silence is such an indispensable condition for communication, in fact, that Erving Goffman, in his theory of social interaction, posits that every dialogic situation is structured by taking "turns at talk."[29]

We are speakers only to the extent that we are listeners at the same time, and Pope Francis pays constant attention to this dichotomy. Indeed, even Pope Benedict XVI addressed this particular subject in a way that brought together communication, spirituality, and knowledge:

> Silence is an integral element of communication; in its absence, words rich in content cannot exist. In silence, we are better able to listen to and understand ourselves; ideas are born and acquire depth; we understand with greater clarity what it is we want to say and what we expect from others; and we choose how to express ourselves.... When messages and information are plentiful, silence becomes essential if we are to distinguish what is important from what is insignificant or secondary. Deeper reflection helps us to discover the links between events that at first sight seem unconnected, to make evaluations, to analyze messages; this makes it possible to share thoughtful and relevant opinions, giving rise to an authentic body of shared knowledge. For this to happen, it is necessary to develop an appropriate environment, a kind of "eco-system" that maintains a just equilibrium between silence, words, images, and sounds.[30]

As St. Augustine reminds us, "our souls need solitude. In solitude, if the soul is attentive, God shows himself. The crowd is noisy; to see God, silence is necessary."[31] But silence is not just meditation and listening; as in Bergoglio's first public appearance, silence can be its own form of communication. The Palo Alto School holds that it is impossible not to communicate,[32] and Paul Watzlawick's study finds that

> in a situation where people are present, "it is impossible not to communicate": even in an anonymous situation (as on a subway train) people send out nonverbal messages (for example, "even though I am a few inches away from you, I'm not threatening and do not wish to invade your personal space"), and other people (fellow travelers) receive the message, confirm it, and reinforce it ("great, likewise for me with regard to you and your space").[33]

In what we do not say, in what we do not do, there is inevitably a meaning, perceptible to whomever we are speaking, and it is not by chance that Roland Barthes spoke of the semiotization of daily realty into a text that could be interpreted according to its various forms and functions.[34]

William Shakespeare, in *Hamlet*, wrote that "words without thoughts never to heaven go" (Act III, Scene 3). Successful communication "is, today as yesterday, today more than yesterday, essentially the fruit of thought but also of creativity and, finally, of a love of silence."[35]

Silence is also a kind of welcome and a quiet meditation, a practice to which St. Francis attributed great importance, as Thomas of Celano attests, who, though not one of his first followers, came to know him personally.

> He always sought a place apart from others where he might become one with his God, not just in spirit but

in his body. And if, by surprise, he felt himself *visited by the Lord*, so as not to remain without a cell, he made one of his own cloak for himself. And if he were at times without one of these, he would cover his face with his sleeve, so as not to reveal the *hidden manna* he was receiving. He would always place something between himself and those standing nearby, so that they might not see his *bridegroom's coming*: thus he was able to pray without being seen, even if he might be in a crush of thousands, as if in the corner of a ship. And if, in the end, none of this was possible, he made a temple of his chest. Absorbed into God, unconscious of his own self, he neither sighed nor coughed. His breathing was still and all other external signs disappeared.[36]

If in Francis of Assisi this welcoming in of God represents an indispensable moment of leaving reality behind without ever becoming a goal in and of itself, this same vision comes forward again in Bergoglio. By considering listening, prayer, and meditation fundamental, he protects himself from drifting away into any sort of solipsism that might take him out of reality and into isolation from others, all of which would be the negation of communication, for, as the original Latin root word suggests, *communicare*, "to hold in common," "to share," implies instead a going out from oneself. One cannot *not* communicate, therefore, and for Pope Francis, this exchange with others becomes both an essential dimension of living as well as of his pastoral work.

Like the saint from Assisi, Bergoglio, too, is convinced that a simple, straightforward way of speaking is an indispensable tool for a Church with a mission to go out into the world:

The Church was born catholic, that is to say that she was born "outward-bound," that she was born missionary. Had the apostles remained in the upper room, without going out to disseminate the Gospel, the Church would be the Church of only that people, of that city, of that upper room. But they all went out into the world, from the moment of the Church's birth, from the moment the Spirit descended on them. And this is why the Church was born "outward-bound," that is, missionary. This is what we express by deeming her *apostolic*, because an apostle is one who spreads the Good News of the resurrection of Jesus. . . . If, for example, some Christians . . . say: "We are the chosen ones, we alone," in the end, they die. They die first spiritually, then they die bodily, because they have no life, they are not capable of generating life, other people, other peoples: they are not apostolic. And it is precisely the Spirit who guides us to meet our brothers, even those who are most distant in every sense, in order that they may share with us the gift of love, peace, and joy that the Risen Lord has bequeathed us.[37]

The debt Bergoglio owes to St. Francis will become explicit with the publication of the encyclical letter

Laudato si', in which the reference to St. Francis's poem *Cantico delle creature* is its very title. In the section dedicated to the figure of St. Francis, Bergoglio points out the reasons he chose him as a model: "The poverty and austerity of Saint Francis were no mere veneer of asceticism, but something much more radical: a refusal to turn reality into an object simply to be used and controlled."[38] As we will see later, even in his choice of themes, one hears an echo of St. Francis. In fact, Bergoglio seems to have taken up these themes, at the very heart of the holy man of Assisi's ministry, and gone about updating them for today's world:

> the intimate relationship between the poor and the fragility of the planet, the conviction that everything in the world is connected, the critique of new paradigms and forms of power derived from technology, the call to seek other ways of understanding the economy and progress, the value proper to each creature, the human meaning of ecology, the need for forthright and honest debate, the serious responsibility of international and local policy, the throwaway culture and the proposal of a new lifestyle.[39]

His declared intention found in the Introduction is significant: "I would like to enter into dialogue with all people about our common home"[40]—which puts forward the notion of dialogue quite explicitly, which is quite unique for a written (rather than spoken) text and particularly for a text of such importance as an encyclical. Indeed, as we will see more fully in what follows, in his writings, too, Pope

Francis consistently emphasizes a call to oral expression, a preference for speech, which Barthes called "degree zero" of writing,[41] or, as another Jesuit, Walter Ong, saw it,[42] representing a kind of secondary recovery of oral expression. This choice, arising from a nature in continuous movement toward speech and thus toward change, brings us neatly to that other point of reference that shaped his religious formation, namely, St. Ignatius of Loyola.

Ignatian Discernment

The second key piece to appreciate about Pope Francis's communication style, another aspect of his past in which it is rooted, is his formation as a Jesuit, his immersion in Ignatius's way of life:

> His ministry as bishop, his way of acting and thinking, is shaped by the Ignatian *visio*, by the paradoxical tension of being always and everywhere in *actione contemplativus*. If one does not place Bergoglio's actions into this frame of contemplative, profoundly prayerful discernment, then one cannot understand their meaning. Pietro Favre, whom Francis has proclaimed a saint, remains always and in all situations his model: a man who wove Ignatian discernment into the very fiber of his being and acting in world.[43]

This spirituality of St. Ignatius is what reconciles two different aspects of faith: a respect for the absolute freedom and uniqueness of the human person while still honoring the requirement of obedience, understood as assent to the faith. The Church stands between both: it recognizes spiritual giftedness, in itself and in others, and at the same time, it consents in filial obedience to being molded and shaped. The core of Ignatian discernment is based, therefore, on fidelity to the Church, on one's personal readiness to engage in formation by undertaking the spiritual exercises, through a mystagogic journey in which one draws close to the paschal mystery of the resurrected Christ, through a liturgical understanding and practice, and then by witnessing to one's own faith in one's real, everyday life.

In his *Spiritual Exercises*, St. Ignatius of Loyola puts forward the rules of discernment, a way of rediscovering, in the midst of a chaotic reality, the certainty of what is good, so as to know the good and live it fully and thereby arrive at "spiritual consolation" through a profound renewal of life. When we are in a state of "spiritual desolation," that is, distant from the presence of God, we feel discouraged and disoriented. By contrast, we are in a state of spiritual consolation when we find ourselves living in a way that is close to the Holy Spirit, who communicates to us what is of God. It isn't difficult to see in this sort of spiritual training one very important element of Pope Francis's pastoral approach, namely, his notion of change through adversity. Spiritual discernment often comes into play for us in times of change or growth, when passing from one stage of life to another; and in so many ways, today's world is exactly such a period. For this reason, too, because of his simple, grounded way of communicating, he is a pope perfectly "syntonic" with our times, apt for our "liquid" society[44] that is in a constant state of development and is always seeking a new state of equilibrium. In many of his public statements and addresses, as we will see in detail, he emphasizes this concept of change.

"For new wine, new wineskins. This is the newness of the Gospel." Francis then asked, "What does the Gospel bring us? Joy and newness." However, he continued, "these doctors of the law were locked up in their commandments, in their rules." So much that "St. Paul, speaking about them, tells us that before faith came—that is, Jesus—we were all held as prisoners under the law. But this law was not cruel: held but as prisoners, waiting for faith to come. Indeed, that faith which would be revealed in Jesus himself."[45]

Over against a blind obedience to the law, Pope Francis affirms the clarifying power of the Gospel's newness, as well as our ability to read and interpret it so we might acquire the discernment needed to guide us toward what is good: a true hermeneutic in which we believe and grow in the faith.

Let us call to mind here the first rule of the spiritual exercises written by Ignatius of Loyola:

In the persons who go from mortal sin to mortal sin, the enemy commonly proposes to them apparent pleasures, making them imagine sensual delights and pleasures in order to hold them more and make them grow in their vices and sins. In these persons the good spirit uses the opposite method, pricking

them and biting their consciences through the process of reason.[46]

These very words show their affinity with the way Pope
Francis goes about communicating, particularly in his
capacity to read reality so as to "prick and bite" one's conscience toward a renewal of life. We will see him return to
this theme over and over again in reference to the Church
itself, for example, in his talk in July 2015, on the occasion
of the national convocation of the Renewal in the Holy
Spirit Movement that took place in St. Peter's Square: "The
river must be lost in the ocean. Yes, if the river comes to a
halt the water becomes stagnant."[47] The river is made up of
movements within the Church, says the pope in so many
words, all of which have a duty to move outward, opening
themselves up to the world and establishing relationships.
A Church that does "not end in the ocean of God, in the
love of God . . . would work for itself and this is not of Jesus
Christ; this is of the Evil One, of the father of lies. The
Renewal continues, it comes from God and goes to God."[48]

We find ourselves here immersed in a Christological
and Christocentric vision of the faith which requires the
faithful to continually ask God for the "grace of memory."
Renewal is neither giving up nor forgetting but rather a
movement forward in continuity with the past: we must
always carry forward within us the memory of that first
encounter with Christ in which "life was changed" in a way
that is then lived out daily through sharing and encounter.
It would be good to

"take up the Gospels" and read again the many accounts there in order "to see how Jesus encounters the people, how he chooses the apostles." And realize, perhaps, that some encounters "resemble mine," for "each one has her own" encounter. Thus, the pope offered two practical and concrete suggestions "that will do us good." First of all "pray and ask for the grace of memory." And then ask yourself: "When, Lord, was that encounter, that love I had at first?" In order "not to feel the rebuke that the Lord gives in Revelation: 'I have this against you, that you have abandoned the love you had at first.'" The pope's second suggestion was to "take up the Gospel and see Jesus' many encounters with so many different people." It is obvious, he explained, that "the Lord wants to encounter us. He wants a face-to-face relationship with us." For certain, "in our life there was a strong encounter that led us to change our life somewhat and to be better."[49]

Pope Francis reads Ignatius thus:

One maxim that always struck me from Ignatius's vision: *Non coerceri a maximo, sed contineri a minimo divinum est.* I have often reflected on this phrase with regard to leadership and governance: do not expand to take up a lot of space but rather take up as little space as possible. The virtue of this balance between big and small is magnanimity, staying right in the middle, that place where one can always spot the horizon. It's doing small things every day with a big heart open to

God and to others. It's valuing the little things within the vast expanse that is the Kingdom of God.[50]

An apparently ordinary and everyday process, it would first appear, but which in reality is not at all easy, and which brings forth spiritual fruit only when we devote ourselves to learning from the world we find around us. This insight is reflected in how Pope Francis uses the example of simple daily choices in his way of speaking:

Such discernment takes time. Many, for example, believe that change and reform can happen quickly. I believe that time is needed to put into place the bases for true and effective change. This time is one of discernment. And sometimes discernment actually leads one to do right away what one thought one might not do until much later. That is what happened to me in my first few months as pope. Discernment always comes about through the presence of the Lord, watching for signs, paying attention to what is happening, listening to people, particularly the poor. My choices, even those that have to do with my daily life, like driving an ordinary car, are all connected to a process of spiritual discernment that is dictated by the people and things around me, the signs of the times around me. My discernment in the Lord guides my leadership.[51]

St. Ignatius's teachings are one of the cornerstones of Pope Bergoglio's life, just as are the teachings of St. Francis.

Both share a close connection between a renewal of the spirit and acting with integrity in the world, and they each reflect a dimension of exchange and dialogue, because, as linguist Wilhelm von Humboldt put it, "all speaking is based on dialogical exchange."[52] However, this complete openness to one's neighbor, and the foundation of trust and transparency that it requires, is not devoid of risks nor of potential problems, among which: gossip.[53]

The Communication Ecology of Pope Francis

Any message, in the course of passing from sender to receiver, is subject to some form of interference. From the very first theories concerning communications,[54] the informational paradigm elaborated and proposed by the father of linguistics, Roman Jakobson,[55] up to the more relational model proposed by Umberto Eco,[56] there has been a progressive clarification of how important the moment of decoding is, that time when a message is interpreted, which can lead to a discussion—or a crisis—depending on what forms of interference are present, which are in their turn connected to various factors, such as the means of communications or one's interpretive schema.[57]

It is not hard to see how this latter—one's interpretative schema—becomes in fact a crucial matter when we are dealing with a message of global significance such as a statement from the pope: for, the schema applied to interpret what he said, which itself varies widely according to one's social context, can be at great odds from the schema out of which the message came originally. And even if we set aside the matter of social context, various ideological schemata can likewise corrupt the meaning of a message, even messages as deliberately straightforward as that of Pope Francis. His commitment to grounding what he says in factual truth and in the lived reality of relationship is unwavering, and he does so using modes of communication that we will examine more thoroughly in the chapters to follow here. But this very same transparency of his, which he follows rigorously, allows a parallel message at times to be created, which, like a cancer cell, changes and multiplies, nourishing itself on secrets, slander, and gossip.

Here we recall the famous anecdote in which Socrates turns to a friend who is about to share a dark secret about someone else with him and stops him first with the following question: "Has your intention passed through the three filters?" And when his friend asked him what he was talking about Socrates explained: "First, are you sure what you are about to tell me is true? Second, are you sure what you are about to tell me is something good about the person? Third, are you sure that what you are telling me will be useful for me to know?" At which point, his friend held his tongue.

Saint Ignatius is very clear that the gray area of secrets and intrigues is one of the principal places that "the enemy" operates to successfully pull a soul away from the pursuit of goodness:

> Likewise, the enemy acts as a licentious lover in wanting to be secret and not revealed. For, as the licentious man who, speaking for an evil purpose, solicits

a daughter of a good father or a wife of a good husband, wants his words and persuasions to be secret, and the contrary displeases him much, when the daughter reveals to her father or the wife to her husband his licentious words and depraved intention, he easily gathers that he will not be able to succeed with the undertaking begun: in the same way, when the enemy of human nature brings his wiles and persuasions to the just soul, he wants and desires that they be received and kept in secret; but when one reveals them to his good confessor or to another spiritual person who knows his deceits and evil ends, it is very grievous to him, because he gathers, from his manifest deceits being discovered, that he will not be able to succeed with his wickedness begun.[58]

Ill disposed to malicious secrets or gossip, Pope Francis consistently chooses immediacy and clarity of communication when faced with problematic situations—hence his nickname, "the phone-call pope." Indeed, the telephone is one method he uses to enact the simple, personal touch he prefers in his communications, but it also provides a way to reduce any interference as much as possible, given that it is the mode of exchange as direct as humanly possible—literally, person to person.

More than once he has spoken about this area of concern, emphasizing how tongue wagging, chatter, and gossip can be weapons that insinuate themselves into the everyday life of the community, sowing envy, jealousy, and a craving for power. In welcoming pilgrims from El Salvador, Pope Francis makes reference to what befell their fellow countryman, Monsignor Oscar Romero, who was killed in 1980 for his denunciation of the violence perpetrated by the military regime in power at the time:

> Archbishop Romero's martyrdom did not occur precisely at the moment of his death; it was a martyrdom of witness, of previous suffering, of previous persecution, until his death. But also afterward because, after he died—I was a young priest and I witnessed this—he was defamed, slandered, soiled, that is, his martyrdom continued even by his brothers in the priesthood and in the episcopate. I am not speaking from hearsay; I heard those things. In other words, it is nice to see him like this: as a man who continues to be a martyr. I think that now they would no longer say such things. However, after giving his life, he continued to give it, allowing himself to be scourged by all of that misunderstanding and slander. This gives me strength, God only knows. Only God knows the history of people and how many times people who have already given their life, or who have died, continue to be scourged with the hardest stone that exists in the world: the tongue.[59]

Chatter and gossip were such lethal weapons that they ended up making the archbishop an inconvenient priest, so inconvenient that on March 24, 1980, a flurry of gunfire murdered him at the moment he was elevating the chalice in consecration. But inconvenient to whom? Certainly not to the poor or the marginalized, certainly not to those who, throughout that tortured country, held the cross before them as a sign of hope and a promise of new and greater respect for human dignity. The Gospel, when preached with courage until blood is shed, cannot be anything other than inconvenient to certain groups, to a way of thinking that always seeks compromise and accommodation. Threatened many times for having taken a stand against the regime, when counseled to be prudent or to travel with bodyguards, Romero would answer: "I have my cross upon my chest, I have nothing to fear." And his pectoral cross was silver, because he had given his gold cross to pay for the expenses of a trial of a young man being persecuted by the government. As both pastors and communicators, there are more than a few points of similarity between Romero and Pope Francis.

In a homily given at morning Mass at Santa Marta, inspired by a story of Jesus' life in Nazareth as well as the Gospel of Luke, Bergoglio reflects on how "one can see what our soul is like" and how it can be swayed one way or another by the winds of gossip. In Nazareth, the pope explained:

> All were waiting for Jesus. Everyone wanted to meet him because they had heard of all he had done in Capernaum, the miracles. And when the ceremony began, they asked their guest to read from the Book. Jesus did so and read from the book of the prophet

Isaiah, which was a prophecy about him. It was for this reason that he ended his reading with the words: "Today this scripture has been fulfilled in your hearing."[60]

The first reactions among those listening, Francis goes on to say, were the most beautiful: they appreciated his words and made them their own. Nevertheless, slowly, Francis goes on to say, the worm of envy began to insinuate itself into the mind of a certain man who began to ask questions: "Where did this man study? Is this not Joseph's son? And we all know to whom he is related? What university did he go to?"—such that the people around him turned on Jesus, putting him to the test. As the pope puts it, "They wanted a show. 'Work a miracle and we will all believe in you!'; but Jesus is not a performing artist."[61]

And finally, in an epilogue to this incident:

They became angry. They stood up and led Jesus to the brow of the hill that they might thrown him down to kill him. What had begun in joy almost ended in crime, out of jealousy, out of envy. This isn't just about 2,000 years ago, it happens every day, in our heart, in our communities. We might welcome someone and speak well of him the first day, but little by little that worm eats away at our minds until our gossip banishes him from good opinion. The person in a community who gossips against his or her neighbor is, in a sense, killing him.[62]

His indefatigable insistence on transparency and direct-
ness could well be considered atypical for our time. Without question, the symbolic world in which our age unfolds
is distinctly at odds with any norms of honest or transparent communication. In fact, some of the cultural norms
that define our postmodern society are based rather on
misinterpretation, on a recursive *mise en abîme*, on fluidity
of role and intentional distortion.[63] In particular, gossip
serves an important function because it helps us to define
and reinforce our role and our identity: "Starting with
unverified information (at times deliberately introduced
into the informational cycle), each subject (receiving it and
passing it on) uses it as material to construct or redefine
one's own individual relationship to others."[64]

This contrast between postmodern communication
practices and Church teaching could not be more stark.
To talk about something true, perhaps in good faith, perhaps not, by adding this detail or that detail which then
starts to move the basic facts further and further from the
truth fully corresponds to what biblical language describes
as using a "lying tongue" and engaging in slander, as over
against the Word of God, which requires we rid ourselves
"of all malice and all deceit, hypocrisy, envy, and slander
of every kind" (1 Pet 2:1). Such sincerity and clarity are, of
course, not easy to maintain within contemporary society,
in which there are many justifications for lies in the service of the good in order to conceal dangerous truths or
circumstances about which an obfuscating silence is maintained. In other words, we now live in a world in which

political action finds itself at odds with spiritual action, in which the vagueness of a phrase like "one might say that" is used to manage situations or resolve crises.

Its usefulness, in fact, and not just sheer human perversity, is the reason that gossip enjoys such popularity within our contemporary culture and has fueled a veritable explosion of online platforms for sharing it throughout the world of social media. Gossip is "a socially structured modality that produces and transmits meaning . . . a type of discourse premised by necessity upon its social distribution, many-sided, needing collective collaboration and thus diffusive interest in order to work."[65]

In short, it is a form of communication that depends on the active collaboration of a gossiper (or more than one, as the case may be) and a surrounding environment that is not merely receptive but is reflective and diffusive. Gossip wouldn't be effective, after all, if each one of us wasn't somehow and in some way involved in spreading it around. From an anthropological perspective, the profile of a gossiper shows a desire for power within his or her own community, a leader, someone who makes the rules, someone who stands in judgment. Gossips set themselves up as caretakers for the values and integrity of their own communities, and the highest source of their pleasure is when they succeed at this task. Gossips spare no one and relish exercising the peculiar power they wield over their own.

Which is why the struggle against gossip undertaken by Pope Francis, far from outdated, ends up being very much of our own time. For a pope with such an obvious conviction that form should reflect substance, distortions of communication clearly therefore reflect a distortion in the use of power. If speaking is also an action, as John L. Austin maintained,[66] then never is a *flatus vocis* without meaning nor harmless but instead may well be characterized as an act of authentic violence. "Words are our tools and, as a minimum, we should use clean tools: we should know what we mean and what we do not, and we must forearm ourselves against the traps that language sets us."[67]

Pope Francis has had personal experience on a number of occasions with many such traps, having often been in the direct line of fire of slander and gossip both within and outside the Church. Thus, his promotion of plain-speaking and truth does not come at all from some idealistic demand for a tidy purity to serve as a shield against an impure and messy contemporary social context. Rather, it is his invitation to act: by making things happen with his words, or even more precisely, by bringing light with his words, Pope Francis is acting against any who would (or would try to) bend language to their own purposes by way of that abuse of language which is gossip.

We call to mind the time in which "it was said" that the Bishop of Carpi, Monsignor Francesco Cavina, had complained about the excessive media presence of the pope which was stealing attention from the work of local churches and their pastors, all of whom were fulfilling their ministerial calling out of the range of the lights and cameras. The pope didn't ask how, what, or why: he simply picked up the phone and called Monsignor Cavina, "as a sign of renewed respect, trust, and affection for him," which, when made public, stopped the slander from continuing to be spread. This kind of spontaneity in conversation, clear and sincere, puts an end to any sort of manipulation. And it was the pope himself who invited Monsignor Cavina to make the substance of the phone call public, which, as a press release from the diocese of Carpi put it, "so that this sort of gossip might clearly be discouraged. Monsignor Francesco Cavina expresses his gratitude to the pope for his accessibility and for the encouragement offered in support of his ministry."

The most painful and personal sort of gossip was at the heart of another quite serious incident, in October 2015, when, in the middle of the work of the Synod, front pages around the world proclaimed that the pope was gravely ill. At this "assault" upon him, he reacted promptly as usual with an immediate denial through the official news outlet of the Holy See. Thus, *L'Osservatore Romano* wrote on October 21, 2015: "The moment chosen for starting this brouhaha reveals the manipulative intention behind it."[68] And in addition to this statement was added the voice of Father Federico Lombardi, director of the Vatican Press Office, who declared: "I've issued a denial and I confirm it categorically after verification from many sources, including the Holy Father himself. No Japanese doctor came to the Vatican. No tests were done, such as were indicated in the article. Nor were there airplanes or helicopters. I can confirm that, other than some minor problems with his legs, the pope is in good health."

Now, of course, gossip and disinformation, as well as constant speculation about ulterior motives, are constants within the history of the Church, right from the beginning. Pope Francis knows this well: "We are used to gossip, to the spreading of rumors, and we often transform our communities as well as our family into 'hell' where this kind of crime leads to killing one's brother and sister with one's tongue!"[69] These are not idle words. These are words that confirm once more his conception of communication—and by extension, of society—in which truth entails responsibility.

Francis has pulled no punches in denouncing, *in prima persona*, in the strongest possible terms of censure, the ways in which the institutional Church has lost its way, for example, when thundering against the "businessmen's Church," or emphasizing, as he did in an interview with the Dutch street magazine *Straatnieuws,* that "it's not okay for a believer to talk about poverty or homelessness and then go about living a Pharaoh's lifestyle."[70] Such statements are not a matter of giving scandal or "making news," but, rather, the exact opposite: it is Francis seeking clarity and integrity, aligning church teaching with lived behavior so as *not* to give scandal, so as to rob scandal of its power through the strength of the true word, that word which, above all worldly communications, is the word of the Gospel.

In one of his homilies—that daily synthesis of the relationship between reality and the Gospel word—we see him lay bare the beating heart of Christianity as he understands it, which we might characterize as his recommendation for "less telenovela, more Gospel"

"How do I contemplate with today's Gospel?" And, sharing his personal experience, he proposed the first reflection: "I see that Jesus was in the midst of the crowd, there was a great crowd around him. The word 'crowd' is used five times in this passage. But doesn't Jesus rest? I can imagine: always with the crowd! Most of Jesus' life is spent on the street, with the crowd. Doesn't he rest? Yes, once: the Gospel says that he slept on the boat, but the storm came and the disciples woke him. Jesus was constantly among the people." For this reason, the pope suggested, "we look to Jesus this way, I contemplate Jesus this way, I imagine Jesus this way. And I say to Jesus whatever comes to my mind to say to him. . . . And with this, he continued, "we allow hope to grow, because we have our eyes fixed on Jesus." Then he proposed: "pray in contemplation." And even if we have many commitments, he said, we can always find the time, even fifteen minutes at home: "Pick up the Gospel, a short passage, imagine what is happening and talk to Jesus about it. This way your eyes will be fixed on Jesus, and not so much on soap operas, for example: your ears will be fixed on the words of Jesus and not so much on the neighbors' gossip."[71]

What Francis inveighs against here is the amount of time we waste chattering about inconsequential matters, and, instead, he invites us to read the Gospel every day, to engage in constant conversation with the Lord. One doesn't need God to "be optimistic, stay positive," but true hope "is learned by keeping our eyes fixed on Jesus."[72] Francis's approach is pragmatic, based as it is on a deep awareness that the mechanisms of communication are vulnerable to distortion but can be "restored to health" by way of a greater truth.

For the pope, there are no strangers. Strangers exist only when there are borders, but when borders can be crossed, then they become signs of a productive diversity. Authentic unity presupposes, in fact, the existence of multiplicity. "Living life on the edge," so to speak, which is what makes it possible to cross these boundaries and enables communication between people of all types without losing the richness of difference and diversity, this "life on the edge" is one of the hallmarks of Francis's way of communicating. A relational rationale stands behind his approach. Within his perspective of pluralism and tolerance, our own individual visions of the world, rather than being exclusive of one another, instead come together, by virtue of sharing, as an ideal point of reference, an overriding principle of respect for the dignity of each human being.

Francis also knows quite well that the more that people are given an opportunity to speak with one another, to get to know one another and to understand one another, the more likely it is that they come to that mutual understanding that leads to solidarity and eventually to justice and peace. And the peace that the pope invokes is not simply an "absence of war." The cornerstones upon which peace is founded and about which he speaks make clear what he means by peace, the values that inspire it and nourish it: justice, charity, and mercy. There can be no peace without these three preconditions.

That Francis communicates daily in word, gesture, and meaning flows from the way he understands his pastoral role, renewed in the spirit of St. Ignatius and lived authentically in the spirit of St. Francis. In the next chapters, we will examine in greater detail certain ways his "style of communication" is expressed and what they each mean.

Two

Language and Communication

Do you know what title should be used of the pope? "Servant of the servants of God." It's a little different from the stars. Stars are beautiful to look at. I like to look at them in the summer when the sky is clear. But the pope must be—must be—the servant of the servants of God. Yes, in the media this is happening but there's another truth. How many stars have we seen that are extinguished and fall! It is a fleeting thing. On the other hand, being servant of the servants of God is something that doesn't pass.[1]

Language Is Form and Time

To return to the roots of one's history does not just mean looking backward or reconstructing a time line; it also, and especially, means giving narrative form to one's existence, to gather up the essence of human time as it develops into a story. As philosopher Paul Ricoeur maintains, in fact, "time becomes human time to the extent that it is organized after the manner of a narrative; narrative, in turn, is meaningful to the extent that it portrays the features of temporal experience."[2]

For Ricoeur, it is particularly thanks to story, that is, to time as *configured* by narrative, that the passage of *prefigured* time in the world becomes the *refigured* time within one's mind, and for this reason, both fictional stories and historical accounts are narrative modes based on the exigencies of truth and on the two operations described by Aristotle: *mimesis*—the imitation or representation of action—and *mythos*—discourse, story, the construction of a plot. Though Aristotle in his *Poetics* does not address the problem of temporality, nevertheless for Ricoeur *mimesis* and *mythos* are inseparable from time and from each other: a story is not an exact copy of reality but is an imitation thereof, and imitation is possible only by way of narrative.

In this sense, when speaking of the "mediation of time and story," Ricoeur underlines the "role that emplotment plays in the mimetic process"[3] and concludes that "emplotment already means birthing the intelligible from the accidental, the universal from the singular, the necessary and likely from the episodic."[4]

Within this work of composition and configuration lies the category of "order," masterfully explored by another philosopher, Michel Foucault, in his work *The Order of Things:* "In every culture there exists, therefore, between the requirements of what we might call ordering codes and thoughts of order the naked experience of order and its ways of being."[5] To speak means, first of all, to give order to discourse. Second, through the creation of forms structured by a representation of reality, narrative gives form to the world and gives meaning to our presence in the world itself. Thus, by creating themselves (and us) in narrative, words become things and satisfy a need. Here we are not referring to that primary need we have for communication in service of survival, nourishment, defense, and participation in social groups from which arise both reproduction and protection, but instead we are speaking of narrative as an instrument that creates shared codes and memory. In this sense, as we saw in the preceding chapter, its most basic and predominant form of narrative is oral, though written discourse these days occupies an enormous amount of space:

> Wherever human beings exist they have a language, and in every instance, a language that exists basically as spoken and heard, in the world of sound. . . . Indeed, language is so overwhelmingly oral that of all the many thousands of languages—possibly tens of thousands—spoken in the course of human history only around 106 have ever been committed to writing to a degree sufficient to have produced literature, and most have never been written at all.[6]

Logos in Western tradition is the source of meaning and the very spark of life itself; the word is eternal and cannot be defined, and yet it provides for existence. As Ernst Cassirer writes, "the richness of the logos which gives form to the universe is reflected in the word that always comes back to go beyond its own limits."[7] This is why the spoken word is Pope Francis's primary category of communication: because *dialogue* implies change and makes it possible.

The pope relies on writing for fundamental messages of noteworthy importance (as in the case of encyclical letters or apostolic exhortations), but when he is before a community of the faithful who has come to meet him, he prefers not to read from a prepared text: nearly always, he sets aside his notes and speaks off the cuff. Among many such occasions, we saw him do this in his meeting with youth in Turin in 2015:

> I forgot to tell you that I will now give you my written remarks. I reviewed your questions, and I wrote something in response; but all of that is not what I talked about, all of that came from my heart; so now I will give my written-remark address to the person in charge, and you can make it public [handing the sheets to the priest in charge of youth pastoral care]. There are so many university students here, but I want to avoid reinforcing the idea that university is only for studying with your head: to be a university student also means to go forth, to go forth in service, to the poor especially! Thank you.[8]

In his meetings as well as in his homilies, one of the narrative modes that Bergoglio employs is that of the fable, a story within a story, sometimes in the form of a parable or an anecdote, whether drawn from sacred texts or from real life, a tale told to the listeners in a colloquial, natural, and direct way, drawing them into the action, making them the main characters.

A wonderful example of this sort of story telling can be found in his morning meditation offered at Santa Marta on September 2, 2013, which we already mentioned in our discussion on gossip, during which Bergoglio tells of Jesus' return to Nazareth, as reported in Luke's Gospel. Reinterpreting the text of the evangelist in the form of a dramatic presentation, Pope Francis recreates the scene for his listeners by using various lines from those among the crowd who were envious of Jesus: "But where did this one study? Isn't he Joseph's son? We know his whole family. What university did he go to?" and again, "Perform a miracle and all of us will believe in you."[9]

A similar modality is used when he puts together a talk from anecdotes drawn from daily life, as when he touched upon the matter of the elderly:

It was said that in one family the grandfather lived with his son, his daughter-in-law, and his grandchildren. But the grandfather had grown old; he had had a stroke. . . . He was old, and when he sat at the table to eat, he would spill a little on himself. The dad was ashamed of his own father, and said: "We can't invite people to our home." So he decided to make a small table in the kitchen for the grandfather to eat at alone. This is how it went. A few days later, he came home from work and found his son—six or seven years old—who was playing with wood, a hammer, and nails. "What are you doing, boy?"—"I am making a small table."—"Why?"—"So that when you are old you will be able to eat alone like grandpa!" Don't be ashamed of the grandfather. Don't be ashamed of the elderly.[10]

Bergoglio's wish to make his listeners the protagonists comes through quite powerfully in a talk he gave at one of his stops during his travels through Bolivia in July 2015:

What can I do, as a collector of paper, old clothes, or used metal, a recycler, about all these problems if I barely make enough money to put food on the table? What can I do as a craftsman, a street vendor, a trucker, a downtrodden worker, if I don't even enjoy workers' rights? What can I do, a farm wife, a native woman, a fisher who can hardly fight the domination of the big corporations? What can I do from my little home, my shanty, my hamlet, my settlement, when I daily meet with discrimination and marginalization? What can be done by those students, those young people, those activists, those missionaries who come to a neighborhood with their hearts full of hopes and dreams, but without any real solution for their problems? They can do a lot. They really can. You, the lowly, the exploited, the poor and underprivileged, can do, and are doing, a lot.[11]

Weaving together evangelical narrative with an informal, everyday way of speaking, as a personal friend would, Pope Francis shows himself to be not only the consummate storyteller but one who shrinks down the distance between life and narrative, bringing his listeners into his symbolic world no matter where they are from. This is how he enters into everyone's heart: he is able to pull away the veil that keeps people apart, believers or not, and to bring them together in conversation. This aspect of his inclusivity is on full display in how he conducts himself at the Angelus, where pilgrims are traditionally greeted. Indeed, every Sunday, while mingling eagerly with the crowd to exchange a few words, engaging conversation with no hint of demand or manipulation Pope Francis takes his leave by wishing them "buon appetito," "have a great dinner," or "have a good Sunday."

So it is that the figure of Pope Francis emerges on a world stage that is characterized for the most part by people shouting and devoid of nuance, a public discourse forced into a particular shape dictated by digital media platforms where the communication that occurs is frenetic, facile, immediate, and yet psychologically quite complex:

> Ours is a culture in which people are inundated by a tremendous flood of information and noise. It is a culture without silence, such that people have become, as Max Picard put it, mere "appendices to the noise." When we look, we see that ours is a culture in which everyone is talking and no one is listening. In fact, our not listening is itself a form of self-defense. We don't listen, or only tune in half way so that we aren't overwhelmed by the thousands of messages that are continually coming at us, that are bursting forth all

the time from all the various media. In the face of such an unwelcome flood, most people's tendency is not to bother with the tiresome work of being selective, thus ending by ignoring both the banal messages coming at us—which is most of them—but also by not listening to those that are on the other hand both interesting and vital.[12]

Italo Calvino, in his *Lezioni americane*, had already talked about this modern linguistic problem:

Sometimes, it appears to me that a genuine plague is being visited upon humanity by way of the very faculty that is its basic characteristic, namely, its use of words, a linguistic plague that manifests itself through a loss of cognitive power and immediacy, with a thoughtless automatism that reduces all expression to its most generic, anonymous, and abstract forms, watering down their meanings, blunting their expressive power, putting out any spark that might result from the encounter of words with new circumstances.[13]

This lack of a "take" on what is real is the product of a violent *logos* that—more in keeping with its original Greek meaning than its subsequent Judeo-Christian elaboration—impairs the freedom and grace of communication, polluting what gets said with a breathless, almost drunken lack of control typified by its incapacity for realism or a faithful representation of reality.[14] In response to this sinister turn that communication has taken in this digital age, there is more than ever a need to return to using words that reverberate with the true meaning of things. Pope Francis communicates effectively, not simply because what he says is simple and unequivocal but also, as he made clear in the apostolic exhortation *Evangelii gaudium*,[15] each of his communicative acts is rooted in his will and desire to faithfully portray what is real through the joy of the Gospel.

Promulgated November 24, 2013, eight months after he was elected to the pontificate, *Evangelii gaudium* anticipates in some ways the themes of the encyclical *Laudato si'*,[16] and dwells at great length on the need for renewal in the Church, envisioning a "Church that goes forth":

> Let us go forth, then, let us go forth to offer everyone the life of Jesus Christ. Here I repeat for the entire Church what I have often said to the priests and laity of Buenos Aires: I prefer a Church that is bruised, hurting, and dirty because it has been out on the streets, rather than a Church that is unhealthy from being confined and from clinging to its own security. I do not want a Church concerned with being at the center and that then ends by being caught up in a web of obsessions and procedures. If something should rightly disturb us and trouble our consciences, it is the fact that so many of our brothers and sisters are living without the strength, light, and consolation born of friendship with Jesus Christ, without a community of faith to support them, without mean-

ing and a goal in life. More than by fear of going astray, my hope is that we will be moved by the fear of remaining shut up within structures that give us a false sense of security, within rules that make us harsh judges, within habits that make us feel safe, while at our door people are starving and Jesus does not tire of saying to us: "Give them something to eat" (Mark 6:37).[17]

I will be dedicating part of the next chapter to examining both these documents in greater detail with the intention of exploring their linguistic and communicative aspects more fully, since, although they are written texts, they very much fall into the category of the pope's "linguistic acts," a category introduced by John L. Austin in his work *Speech Act Theory*,[18] according to which all behavior on the part of a speaker is understood as action.

Austin and a number of other twentieth-century thinkers devoted a great deal of attention to this relational aspect of communication, thereby making language one of the central themes of modern philosophy. Among the many aspects of language explored philosophically is that of dialogue, so dear to the heart of Pope Francis, for it is dialogue that allows what would be "simple" communication to become instead a category of entering-into-relationship and thus, by extension, of spirituality, insofar as this relational dialogue engages the mystery of the divine.

His relationship with the faithful is always a dialogue, a reciprocal exchange, a meeting in which the pope offers not just a spoken message of God's mercy but his own presence and closeness as well. In his turn, every time, he asks that they pray for him and that they live according to Jesus' teachings, a request that passes over the unimportant so as to focus the person he's speaking with on what is truly essential: "within the immediacy of relationship all that is mediated becomes irrelevant."[19] When truly *word*, and not mere chatter, the word is that place of an encounter from which all instrumentalization and objectification are excluded, thereby reaching the ineffable, authentic realm of grace. "I meet the other, Thou, by grace—not through my own seeking. And speaking to Thee, the other, is an essential act of my being."[20]

But what are the words spoken (and more important, the nature of the speaker) that characterize the communications of Pope Francis? We live in a mass-media culture that shapes our attitudes and our values. The pope is aware of this: if one were to claim, in some way, that Christians are not a part of this culture and are not subject to the tensions and pressures that the world puts on people, then Christians would have little to say to society as a whole and would only be able to talk to one another. Pope Francis, on the other hand, speaks clearly about the wonders of God with words and gestures that have an arresting depth and richness drawn from his own life experience, in this way opening up for every man or woman he meets possibilities of new visions and paths forward.

The primary message Pope Bergoglio brings forward is the Gospel of mercy. In today's world, we are witnessing "a passage from boundless trust to an equally boundless diffidence toward the future,"[21] and in this context, Pope Francis uses the experience of encounter and his closeness to others to establish a paradigm of meaning that can lead to unexpected glimpses of paradise for the distracted and the disinterested, all of which would be impossible, using the traditional rhetoric of judgment, with those who have lost interest or fallen away.

Figures of the Word: Metaphor and Symbolism in a Strategy of Inclusion

We have seen how, right from the start, Pope Francis's simplicity is a key piece of his communication.[22] "Simplicity of speech," however, does not mean "poverty of speech," for both his vocabulary as well as his rhetorical and symbolic resources are quite rich. And yet, the Gospel itself is a narrative cast in very simple language which is at the same time profound, in its own right, and so, similarly, Bergoglio takes up a conversational approach, adopting a friendly, familiar[23] tone, full of references to normal, everyday life while still taking full advantage of various, quite effective rhetorical devices. One such technique, in particular, is his use of analogies, metaphors, and similarities, which, as Foucault reminds us in his analysis of the medieval theory of similitude, is among the oldest and the most powerful.[24]

In the end, what today's world of communication shares in common with the medieval imagination is that it, too, is dense with symbols that point back and forth to one another such that the endless play of signification, which the philosopher of language Charles S. Peirce once called the "fugue of interpretants,"[25] runs the risk of hiding, confusing, or fracturing the message. Pope Francis is very aware of this real danger, so he takes care that the metaphors and analogies with which he peppers his talks are always tied to simple, concrete images easily and quickly visualized by the mind's eye. "Be shepherds, with the 'odor of the sheep,' make it real," he said, for example, during the Chrism Mass in 2013, celebrating his first Good Friday as pope.[26] Or again, some months later, on the vigil of Pentecost, "We cannot become starched Christians, those overeducated Christians who speak of theological matters as they calmly sip their tea. No!"[27] Moreover, in his first interview published in *La civiltà cattolica*, Bergoglio detailed his vision, that of a Church like a "field hospital,"[28] a comparison that would pop up again in subsequent talks:

> The priest is called to learn this, to have a heart that is moved. Priests who are—allow me to say the word— "aseptic," those "from the laboratory," all clean and tidy, do not help the Church. Today we can think of the Church as a "field hospital." Excuse me but I repeat it, because this is how I see it, how I feel it is: a "field hospital." Wounds need to be treated, so many wounds! So many wounds! There are so many people who are wounded by material problems, by scandals, also in the Church. . . . People wounded by

the world's illusions.... We priests must be there, close to these people. Mercy first means treating the wounds.[29]

So, it is not mere happenstance that on numerous occasions Bergoglio uses the metaphor of the "flesh" of Christ in making reference to his humanity, to his Incarnation, when he speaks of the experience of those who suffer: "Do not be afraid to draw near to the flesh, to the flesh that hungers and thirsts, to the flesh that is sick and wounded, to the flesh that atones for its guilt, to the flesh without clothes to wear, to the flesh that knows the corrosive bitterness of that loneliness born of contempt."[30] Again, on the Vigil of Pentecost, in reflecting on the giving of alms, he called again for drawing near to those who suffer:

> We must become courageous Christians and go in search of the people who are the very flesh of Christ, those who are the flesh of Christ!
>
> So, when I go to hear confessions—I mean, I can't really do that now, hear confessions, given where I am, but that's another problem—when I *used* to go to hear confessions in my previous diocese, people would come to me and I would always ask them: "Do you give alms?"—"Yes, Father!" "Very good." And I would ask them two further questions: "Tell me, when you give alms, do you look the person in the eye?" "Oh I don't know, I haven't really thought about it." The second question: "And when you give alms, do you touch the hand of the person you are giving

them to or do you toss the coin at him or her?" This is the problem: the flesh of Christ, touching the flesh of Christ, taking upon ourselves this suffering for the poor. Poverty for us Christians is not a sociological, philosophical, or cultural category, no. It is theological. I might say this is the first category, because our God, the Son of God, abased himself, he made himself poor to walk along the road with us. This is our poverty: the poverty of the flesh of Christ, the poverty that brought the Son of God to us through his Incarnation.[31]

The pope's rhetoric, thus, is no mere improvisation, but, on the contrary, is very intentionally fashioned to have an impact on his listeners:

Pope Francis speaks of the "babysitter Church" (April 17) in disapproval of a Church that simply "takes care of the child to put them to sleep," rather than acting like a mother should with her children; and he speaks of "spray can God" (April 18) to warn against an idea of a God different from a Christian understanding that works fine in any and all situations ... or he speaks of "satellite Christians," as on April 20, to speak against Christians who let themselves be guided by "common sense" and "worldly prudence" rather than by Jesus.[32]

Words are powerful, and he uses them carefully. Thus, in 2015, returning to this theme again during an interview with Rádio Renascença, on the occasion of the *ad limina apostolorum* visit of the Portuguese bishops,[33] Bergoglio explicitly suggests that it represents "prudence to not create a purely theoretical catechesis,"[34] adding that

> Catechism is to provide doctrine for living, and thus, it needs to speak three languages—the language of the head, the language of the heart, and the language of the hands—and the catechist, too, must speak these three languages also, so that a young person can think and know what faith is, but at the same time, feel within the heart what faith is, and at the same time, accomplish things—to think about what one feels and how one acts, to feel what one thinks and what one does, and to act on what one feels and what one thinks.[35]

This unity, this profound coherence of thought, word, and action, is reflected with great precision in the structure of the metaphors and analogies Bergoglio so loves to employ, rhetorical devices characterized by their immediacy, their capacity to spark understanding and integration in whoever hears them, and by how effectively they carry multiple levels of meaning simultaneously. As George Lakoff and Mark Johnson write in their well-known essay that explored the symbolic and performative strength of metaphor—particularly when used politically—metaphor is not merely a question of language. Our cognitive processes as human beings are, for the most part, based on metaphor, which is linked to the fact that our human conceptual system is structured metaphorically. Metaphors—

figures of speech—occur because they are present in a human being's conceptual system.[36] To use a metaphor, therefore, means revealing the very heart of a speaker's thought to establish immediate contact.[37]

Another of Bergoglio's consistent communication techniques is the use of quotations. Like the anecdote, a quotation inserts into the narrative a second level of story and meaning, at the same time clarifying the interpretation and enriching it with further meaning. But beyond that, quotation is also itself a form of sharing, because it simultaneously presumes, creates, and manifests how we all belong to one and the same group, sharing cultural, textural, and experiential codes. To quote something known to the listener is an immediate way to establish mutual recognition and relationship, and to use a quotation not known but referring to a commonly held image is another way of giving of oneself, which we will explore in much more depth as we look at the concept of "gift" within the world of Francis's communication and actions in the next section.

Quotations from the Gospel fit quite naturally into Bergoglio's speeches and talks, of course, but those are not the only citations he uses. He does not hold himself back from drawing wholeheartedly on popular culture. In one homily, for example, he quoted from a song made famous by Mina, *Parole parole,* showing that even the somewhat banal tropes of popular music might be used to make his point. That homily was centered on the theme of loss in relationship to the scandal of arms trading, of all things, and to make his point he employed concepts of great breadth such as peace, reconciliation, and mercy: "each day, when we pray the Our Father, we say: 'forgive us, as we forgive.'" And this, he explained, is in the "'conditional': we are trying to convince God to be good, as we are good in forgiving: in reverse." So, it was in this context that the pope commented: "Words, no? Like she sings in that beautiful song: 'Words, words, words', no? I think the singer is Mina. . . . Words! . . . If you do not forgive, you cannot receive the peace of the Lord, the Lord's forgiveness."[38]

Is referring to such a song frivolous and inappropriate in a homily about such a serious topic? Quite the opposite: using this sort of quotation from popular culture is one way of achieving a greater immediacy of impact on a difficult subject across a broad range of listeners. Hence, similarly, in his speech at the Fifth Convention of the Italian Church, *New Humanism in Jesus Christ*, he adds to the traditional champions of the faith characters from the pen of the popular Italian writer Giovannino Guareschi:

> The Italian Church has great saints whose examples can help her to live the faith with humility, disinterest, and gladness, from Francis of Assisi to Philip Neri. But let us also think of the simplicity of fictional characters such as Don Camillo who was paired with Peppone. It strikes me how in Guareschi's stories the prayer of a good priest merges with the evident closeness to the people. Don Camillo said of himself: "I am a poor, country priest who knows each of his parish-

ioners individually, who loves them, who knows their sorrows and their joys, who suffers and laughs with them." Closeness to the people and prayer are the key to living a popular, humble, generous, and happy Christian humanism. If we lose this contact with the faithful People of God, we lose humanity and we go nowhere.[39]

In playing with well-known references taken from popular culture, Francis is able to speak to believers, to nonbelievers, and to those believers who have been unable to find a Christian identity for themselves. As he puts it:

At times we lose people because they don't understand what we are saying, because we have forgotten the language of simplicity and import an intellectualism foreign to our people. Without the grammar of simplicity, the Church loses the very conditions that make it possible "to fish" for God in the deep waters of his Mystery. . . . Perhaps the Church appeared too weak, perhaps too distant from their needs, perhaps too poor to respond to their concerns, perhaps too cold, perhaps too caught up with itself, perhaps a prisoner of its own rigid formulas, perhaps the world seems to have made the Church a relic of the past, unfit for new questions; perhaps the Church could speak to people in their infancy but not to those come of age. It is a fact that nowadays there are many people like the two disciples of Emmaus; not only those looking for answers in the new religious groups that are sprouting up, but also those who already seem godless, both in theory and in practice. Faced with this situation, what are we to do? We need a Church unafraid of going forth into their night. We need a Church capable of meeting them on their way.[40]

In *Evangelii gaudium*, Bergoglio goes on at some length about the necessity of connecting what one says to the listener's experience and the various contexts in which a conversation about faith is taking place:

> Preachers often use words learned during their studies and in specialized settings that are not part of the ordinary language of their hearers. These are words that are suitable in theology or catechesis, but whose meaning is incomprehensible to the majority of Christians. The greatest risk for a preacher is that he becomes so accustomed to his own language that he thinks that everyone else naturally understands and uses it. If we wish to adapt to people's language and to reach them with God's word, we need to share in their lives and pay loving attention to them.[41]

According to Jakobson's schema, if communication is to work, it requires, first, a context that the receiver can grasp, verbalized or at least verbalizable; second, a common code either partially or entirely shared by sender and receiver; and finally, contact, a physical channel and a connection between sender and receiver that allow them to establish and maintain communication.[42] In such careful attention to the shared content we have seen thus far in the linguistic and communicative choices he makes, we see Pope Francis fully aware of how this model of communication works. Because of his academic studies? Undoubtedly, but we must always remember that Pope Francis's approach to communication[43] grew out of how he was raised and relies on his ability to read the present state of affairs and to look toward the future in the light of the Gospel. He reminds us that the basis of any identification, including linguistic, is an encounter with Jesus and that "focusing on this context can help to make our communication more authentic and humane."[44] In this sense,

> The womb that hosts us is the first "school" of communication, a place of listening and physical contact where we begin to familiarize ourselves with the outside world within a protected environment, with the reassuring sound of the mother's heartbeat.... Today the *modern media*, which are an essential part of life for young people in particular, *can be both a help and a hindrance* to communication in and between families. The media can be a *hindrance* if they become a way to avoid listening to others, to evade physical contact, to fill up every moment of silence and rest.... The media can *help* communication when they enable people to share their stories, to stay in contact with distant friends, to thank others or to seek their forgiveness, and to open the door to new encounters.[45]

For Pope Francis, communication is one of the objectives of evangelization, and both traditional and new media are places made of space and time in which people across all strata of society live and where even the least among us, those rejected or cast off by society, those "who don't belong" also likewise live.[46] As Ernst Cassirer put it, "language is a focal point of one's spiritual being where the lines of our diverse origins come together and from which depart lines of direction toward all areas of the spirit."[47] Whoever is excluded from language, from dialogue and exchange, is thus likewise excluded from the living.

Simplicity and Misunderstanding

We will return to this concept of inclusion, central to both the communicative style and the pastoral practice of Pope Francis, in the section that follows, but first we must attend to the simplicity of language used by this pope so conscientiously, as it pertains to the question of misunderstanding and misuse. It may seem paradoxical that both on the level of semantic and rhetorical choices or in the context of public discourse, maximum simplicity can give rise to some of the most persistent interpretive distortions, but nevertheless, it does.

The first of these distortions is to imagine that every word, every lexical choice, comes from a desire to manipulate. As it is not possible *not* to communicate, obviously every linguistic action carries within it the seed of a more or less conscious intention, which means a pope, well aware of the role he occupies, likewise obviously goes about choosing his words quite carefully. Bergoglio's choice to speak clearly and understandably to the world at large and therefore credibly to the world of nonbelievers beyond the Church has been unfortunately interpreted—in part because of his success—as a kind of "territorial encroachment" and has elicited opposition and criticism on the part of external observers.

In January 2015, in the days following the bloody terrorist attack on the editorial offices of the Parisian satirical magazine *Charlie Hebdo*, the pope was asked for his reaction to what had occurred. So, on a flight from Sri Lanka to the Philippines, he answered a question about the limits of freedom of the press and of satire when it concerns a question of religion:

> Everyone not only has the freedom, the right, but also the obligation, to say what they think in order to promote the common good. The obligation. Think of an elected official, a senator: unless they say what they think is right, they are not working for the common good. Not only these people, but so many others. We have the obligation to speak openly, to enjoy this freedom, but without offending others. It is true one cannot respond violently, but if my good friend Dr. Gasbarri here insults my mother, he'll get punched for it! This is normal! It is normal. We cannot provoke others, we cannot insult their faith, we cannot mock their faith.[48]

The pope's "punch," obviously, was reported within seconds around the world by every news organization and unleashed a storm of comments. In reality, Francis spoke in his own way and said nothing more than the Holy See had always said, namely, that one's right to freedom of thought and expression does not imply a right to insult the religious feelings of believers, a principle asserted with regard to all religious faiths. "Because he said that if someone insults his mother, 'he can expect a punch,' he has been accused of justifying the violence directed by Islamists toward satirical material," says Vatican observer Luigi Accattoli.[49]

And there have been other occasions in which his thoughts have been reduced out of context to mere slogans:

> Nuns who ought to be "mothers, not old maids" (May 8, 2013); Christian life which "isn't spa therapy" (June 15, 2013); the praise of "unbalanced Christians" (September 26, 2013); his deploring "defeated Christians" (April 24, 2014) or those "made up to look like Christians" (December 4, 2014) are expressions that have entertained those listening and garnered praise for the Argentinean's pope's imaginative repertoire. But controversy was brewing and soon arrived in full force.[50]

Nevertheless, Accattoli continues

> Pope Francis keeps his language simple so he can reach ordinary people and those outside.... He is well aware of the many distinctions and nuances that have grown up over the course of the centuries, and he knows their use within academic settings; but he

holds that it is necessary to go beyond them to speak a new language of direct proclamation, person to person, no longer imprisoned by those cultural filters that render it academic or erudite to the listener.[51]

Thus, Bergoglio simplifies his language:

The first effort he makes is to *use images.* In actuality, it isn't really an effort for Francis since he speaks naturally in images, some of which have become famous, starting with the Church as a "field hospital," but also "God-spray," or "pastry-shop Christians," "milkshake faith," "ready-to-wear thought," "or the "babysitter Church." This pope loves illustrations and not just those drawn from religion. Images, in this sense, are for him more powerful than examples. He writes in his first apostolic exhortation, "an attractive image makes the message seem familiar, close to home, practical and related to everyday life. A successful image can make people savor the message, awaken a desire and move the will toward the Gospel" (*Evangelii gaudium* 157). The second effort he makes is to give life to preaching that is "simple, clear, direct, relevant." *Simplicity* is a term applied to the language he uses for he wants to be comprehensible so as not to run the risk of what he says falling upon deaf ears. The pope knows well that whoever has studied theology has learned a refined, technical language that, however, ordinary people don't understand because they are not part of the world of those who talk that way. How can that language be adapted so as to bring the Word to the people? In *Evangelii gaudium*, the pope answers, "If we wish to adapt to people's language and to reach them with God's word, we need to share in their lives and pay loving attention to them" (*Evangelii gaudium* 158). The language of his homilies at Santa Marta is very simple, immediate, comprehensible to anyone. This talent of Francis comes from his life of constant contact with ordinary people [52]

Traditionalists fear that choosing this type of language may sow confusion about what is Christian and fail to provide sufficient direction to the faithful within Catholic circles. Such fears, however, intentionally misconstrue Bergoglio's message, which is, in fact, rather quite plain and uncomplicated, intended to awaken the conscience of believers and to bring in and involve those outsiders who may feel like they have never been heard.

One place crucial to how Pope Francis gets across his overall message is the homily he preaches at morning Mass in the Church of Santa Marta. Here we find, in addition to his usual down-to-earth public presence, his ability to bring the Gospel to life so as to make the truth of the Christian message shine out from behind formulaic obscurity or historical distance:

The strength of a priest is rooted in this relationship, the pontiff added, commenting on the day's Gospel; when Jesus' popularity increased, he went to the Father. As St. Luke recounts: "He withdrew to the wilderness and prayed" (see 5:12-16). Thus, Pope Francis noted, as there was more and more talk about Jesus and large crowds were coming to him to listen to him and be healed, afterward he went to the Father. Thus, he said, Jesus' attitude is a rock of comparison for us who are priests: do we or do we not go to Jesus? A series of questions priests might ask themselves flow from this, the pope said. What place does Jesus Christ have in my life as a priest? Is it a living relationship, disciple to Master, brother to brother, poor man to God? Or is it a bit artificial, like a relationship that doesn't come from the heart? We are united through the Spirit, and when a priest distances himself from Jesus Christ, instead of being anointed [*unto*], he ends up becoming unctuous [*untuoso*]. How greatly do unctuous priests harm the Church! Those who place importance and power in artificial things, in vanities, those who have an affected attitude and way of speaking. How many times, he added, do we hear with dismay: but this is a priest? He seems more like a butterfly because he is always fluttering about vanities and he does not have a relationship with Jesus Christ: he has lost the anointing; he is unctuous.[53]

Particularly in the case of a nonnative speaker like the pope, his play on words is a striking way to focus attention on one of the issues dearest to his heart: the problem of worldly, idolatrous attitudes that lead one astray from a central relationship with Jesus, as embodied in those figures he has called "businessmen-priests" or "priestly entrepreneurs." But the priest "adores Jesus Christ, the priest speaks with Jesus Christ, the priest seeks Jesus Christ, and allows himself to be sought by Jesus Christ. This is the center of our lives. If we do not have this, we lose everything! And then what shall we give to the people?"[54]

With his image of "butterfly priests," the pope gives us a kind of jackalope, a mixed-up creature with a humorous tinge. Francis *castigat ridendo mores*, as Horace puts it in his *Satires*: he censures (bad) habits without mincing words, using neither fancy rhetoric nor verbosity, but neither does he deprive his people of the comfort of an easy laugh. Despite the mocking humor, his serious undertone is clear in his immediate appeal to a deeper message, his calls to what is good as part of our taking personal, moral responsibility for our actions:

> It is beautiful to find priests who have given their lives as priests. Priests of whom the people say: "But yes, he has a bit of a temper, he's got this and that, but he is a priest!" And the people have a nose about these things! Instead, when the people see idolatrous priests, to say it in a word, who instead of having Jesus have their little idols—some are devotees of the god of Narcissus—they say: "poor things!" It is a relationship with Jesus Christ that saves us from worldliness and from the idolatry that makes us unctuous since this

relationship enables us to remain in the anointing. . . .
To you who have so kindly come to concelebrate here
with me, my hope for you is this: lose everything in
life but do not lose this relationship with Jesus Christ.
This is your victory. Onward with this![55]

The Concept of Gift in What Francis Says and Does

Language has both a communicative and a narrative
value, and to these, another yet: a social value. Numerous
anthropological studies, such as those done by Bronislaw
Malinowski,[56] underscore, among other things, the phatic
function of language in the social sense, as a means of creating group cohesion. From a pragmatic point of view, in
social interactions, words are a means of exchange and gift.

The notion of gift as central to the symbolic action of
human beings is, however, a complex and somewhat slip-
pery concept, the interpretation of which depends fundamentally on the context in which it is analyzed. One of
the most insightful essays on gift is by Marcel Mauss,[57] in
which he underscores its ambiguity, justifiably so, given
the basic etymological derivation of the term *gift* whereby
the same word has very different meanings: in English, it
means "offering" and in German, "poison."[58]

In Christianity, the concept of gift is central and has a
positive connotation. Life is a gift (from God to human
beings, from parents to children), as is sacrifice (Jesus'
on the cross, humans' in service of fellowship), and the
notion of gift permeates the Christian tradition, just as it
did previously within Jewish tradition. To give, to receive,

and to reciprocate are all parts of social interaction that is basic to the human experience, but gift as conceived within Christian tradition occurs freely, in contrast to a debt, which, in Mauss's thought, distinctly implies a *duty* and incurs responsibility.

One is not surprised, therefore, that "gift" represents a basic category of Pope Francis's communicative action, especially since unity within the Church and social solidarity are both prominent missions of his pastoral program. Given the range of symbolic approaches possible, here, too, Bergoglio reveals the poetics of characteristic plain-speaking and shows himself as taking advantage of language's symbolic resources throughout his conversations and public statements.

One cunning little example of his symbolism of gift is the *Misericordina*, a "prayer kit," which is handed out now in St. Peter's Square, consisting of a rosary packaged like an over-the-counter medication. And this is how Pope Francis talks about it, focusing precisely on the doubts and questions raised by those with whom he's speaking, framing it all, again, in the form of a dialogue:

> Now I would like to recommend a medicine to you. Some of you may be wondering: "Is the pope a pharmacist now?" It is a special medicine that will help you to benefit from the Year of Faith, as it soon will come to an end. It is a medicine that consists of 59 threaded beads; a "spiritual medicine" called *Misericordina*. A small box containing 59 beads on a string. This little box contains the medicine, and will be dis-

tributed to you by volunteers as you leave the Square. Take them! There is a rosary, with which you can pray the Chaplet of Divine Mercy, spiritual help for our souls and for spreading love, forgiveness, and brotherhood everywhere. Do not forget to take it, because it is good for you. It is good for the heart, the soul, and for life in general! I wish you all a blessed Sunday. Goodbye and have a good lunch![59]

The *Misericordina* ends up being an enormously effective gesture because it makes quite a splash in the news but especially because it takes an abstract concept like "mercy" and makes it immediately comprehensible by using the metaphor of medicine. Mercy is made flesh in an everyday object that anyone, rich or poor, can hold and use. With a single act, a gift, in short, Pope Francis succeeds in bringing together multiple meanings by overlaying the semantics of mercy with those of medication: *necessity* (without mercy, as without a necessary medication, society becomes sick), *saving power* (like medication, mercy makes you better), *efficacy* (mercy works quickly, it has an immediate effect). Here is an idea that seems simple on its face but which carries enormous symbolic complexity underneath, subtly distilled down into a single object.

And again, on April 6, 2014, on the Fifth Sunday of Lent, Pope Francis handed out a pocket-sized collection of the four Gospels to the faithful gathered in St. Peter's Square, using the occasion to talk about his idea of what constitutes a gift:

On recent Sundays I suggested that you all obtain a little Gospel to carry with you throughout the day so that you can read it often. I then thought about an old Lenten tradition in the Church of giving the Gospel to catechumens, to those who are preparing for Baptism. So, today I want to offer you who are here in the Square—but as a sign for all—a pocket-size Gospel. It will be handed out gratis. There are places set up in the Square for distribution. I see them there, there, and there.... Go there and take a Gospel. Take it, carry it with you, and read it every day: It is Jesus himself speaking to you in it! It is the word of Jesus: this is the Word of Jesus!

And like him I say to you: as you have received freely, give freely, pass on the message of the Gospel! Maybe some of you don't think it can be free. "But how much? How much must I pay, Father?" Let's do something: in exchange for this gift, do a charitable action, a gesture of spontaneous love, a prayer for your enemies, an act of reconciliation, something. . . .[60]

An interesting way of presenting what he is doing: the pope here substitutes the idea of exchange (I give you something, you give me something for it) with the idea of giving freely (I give you something without asking anything back, so that you will give something away to someone else without asking for anything back). In the end, it all comes off as quite elementary and obvious, but it is a complete shift of paradigm, pure and simple, that is wholly in accord with the tireless struggle this pope has taken up against greed, stinginess, and the overweening concern about money that has afflicted the Church.

This gift asks of those who receive it that they perform some concrete good work in return that might be, in its way, a message of God's love to others. Just handing out the copies of Gospels themselves is a meaningful enough gesture, from a communications point of view, since they represent the gift of story and word, nothing less than the sacred Word of God, but Pope Francis doing so in the midst of the Lenten season confers upon the act an even greater symbolic significance and power, framing it within the context of that sacrifice *par excellence*, Jesus' death on the cross offered up as a gift to all humanity. Here again we see an ordinary, everyday action—distributing a free booklet—transformed by him into an extraordinarily well-crafted symbolic gift. We do well to note, though, that he neither explains nor makes explicit any of this underlying symbolism: he doesn't want attention to be paid to the craft or cleverness of what he is doing or the multiplicity of meanings his action carries. Quite the contrary, he acts simply, humbly, knowing the crowd probably won't grasp intellectually all the various meanings carried by this gesture, but he counts instead on the fact that they will instinctively "get" what he considers the essential part: go forth, do good, and do it freely.

The following year, he asked "special" volunteers to help him carry out a similar project:

Therefore, in this First Sunday, I thought to give those of you who are here in the Square a small booklet entitled *Custodisci il cuore* ("Guard the heart"). It's this one [he holds up the booklet]. This book contains some of Jesus' teaching and the essential contents of our faith, for example, the seven sacraments, the gifts of the Holy Spirit, the Ten Commandments, the Virtues, the works of mercy, etc. . . . The volunteers, among whom there are many homeless people who have come on pilgrimage, will now distribute them. And as always, today too, here in the Square, are those who are in need, the same ones who bring us a great wealth: the wealth of our doctrine, to guard your heart. Each one of you, take a booklet and carry it with you, as a help for spiritual conversion and growth, which always starts from the heart: the place where the match of daily choices between good and evil is played out, between worldliness and the Gospel, between indifference and sharing. Humanity is in need of justice, of peace, of love and will have it only by returning with their whole heart to God, who is the source of it all. Take the book and read it.[61]

In other words, Bergoglio uses the very people who are the focus of Jesus' ministry in the Gospel—the least among us, the poor, the forsaken—to bring the Word of God forward into the world. With this initiative, translating into concrete action the deeper meaning of Holy Scripture, the pope identifies these people themselves as tangible signs of divine mercy, raising them up as principal actors in the midst of the community and representing the very heart of the Church's mission as envisioned by Pope Francis: a

Church in the streets, open to the world, as he said, like a "field hospital" for those in need.

Like the metaphor of medication, the image of the field hospital also draws us into the semantics of healing, a course of treatment undertaken when wounded and intended to restore health to body and mind. So, once more, in his statement above we encounter another of the multiplicity of meanings inherent in the concept of gift, also deeply tied into its etymology as well, that is, "forgiveness." And with this, the circle of Pope Francis's communicative action is complete, culminating in his decision to declare an Extraordinary Jubilee Year of Mercy, in a straight line from the "medicine" given out in St. Peter's Square. This declaration, with all its enormous practical and doctrinal implications, gives witness to the centrality of his notion of gift within his pastoral ministry.

The Jubilee, we recall, is a designation drawn from Jewish tradition. In Leviticus (25:8-10) we find the commandment to observe a Holy Year or Jubilee every fifty years. During this period, which is one characterized by unlimited generosity founded on complete trust in God's providence, land is left unplanted, contracts are terminated (land and houses returned to their original owners, servants are freed), and, above all, debts are forgiven.

The revolutionary dimension of this practice—both as gift and forgiveness—is obvious, for such an observance in fact sets on its head an entire system of social norms and economic productivity. Indeed, the idea of instituting a genuine Jubilee in contemporary society staggers the mind, but it was no less momentous to simpler societies in ancient times, though we cannot know if—and have good reason to doubt that—such radical provisions were ever fully implemented. One thing that is certain, however, is that "forgiving our debts" in the sense of asking and obtaining pardon for one's sins, is central to the Christian idea of Jubilee, as an event that calls the faithful to gather together in a pilgrimage both literally, physically, and, figuratively, in prayer and meditation. Both make reference to the notion of an open Church, one constantly changing, on the move, holding a hand out to sinners, the special heart's desire of this pope. And in his approach, both the linguistic action—declaring a Jubilee—and the symbolic gesture—opening the Holy Door—constitute twin elements of great power within the complex message he wished to communicate. The Extraordinary Jubilee declared for the year 2016 is understood, in this way, itself as a gift: a gift to the faithful, to the city of Rome, to a world that needs to turn around and reflect on what it lacks.

From Gift to Gesture: Opening, Encounter, and the Social Network

Pope Francis never stops suggesting new ways of moving forward and sees his role as "enzymatic" by activating processes of change through ongoing dialogue with the realities around him. One key piece of this dialogue is another fundamental concept found in the semantics of "gift," namely, "opening."

To give means to open oneself, to oblige oneself to another, to reveal something of oneself and to understand something about the person to whom we are giving, and to expect in return a similar opening, to receive, to welcome the gift. There need not necessarily be any kind of economic exchange, for even when freely given, there is an exchange, a passing between. And openness is one of those subjects Bergoglio especially loves to talk about:

When the Church is closed, she falls sick, she falls sick. Think of a room that has been closed for a year. When you go into it there is a damp smell; many things are wrong with it. A Church closed in on herself is the same, a sick Church. The Church must step outside herself. To go where? To the outskirts of existence, whatever they may be, but she must step out. Jesus tells us: "Go into all the world! Go! Preach! Bear witness to the Gospel!" (see Mark 16:15). But what happens if we step outside ourselves? The same as can happen to anyone who comes out of the house and onto the street: an accident. But I tell you, I far prefer a Church that has had a few accidents to a Church that has fallen sick from being closed. Go out, go out! Do not forget: there must be no question of a closed Church, but rather a Church that is ready to step outside, to go to the outlying regions. May the Lord guide us here on earth.[62]

Through openness, the notion of gift is woven together with service. Often in his public statements and homilies, Pope Francis makes plain his conception of a Church "that goes forth" to serve the Gospel on the margins of society and asserts that the Church fulfills its mission in the world "when the Gospel we preach touches their daily lives, when it runs down like the oil of Aaron to the edges of reality, when it brings light to moments of extreme darkness, to the 'outskirts' where people of faith are most exposed to the onslaught of those who want to tear down their faith."[63]

In these words, we hear the echo of this pontiff's Latin-American religious formation, which he draws on to "infect" the Church with a new charge, inviting pastors, priests, and bishops to "go out, then, in order to experience our own anointing, its power, and its redemptive efficacy: to the 'outskirts' where there is suffering, bloodshed, blindness that longs for sight, and prisoners in thrall to many evil masters."[64] The Church, in his view, must go beyond simply being an institution for the distribution of the sacraments, or worse yet, a depository of ethical rules and moral regulations apart from the real world and its dilemmas. Pope Francis does not consider a "priest who never goes out" a credible pastor: a Church that does not reach out to the outskirts of society offers a model of ministry that ends with "sad priests, in some sense becoming collectors of antiques or novelties, instead of being shepherds living with 'the odor of the sheep.'"[65]

This dimension of openness and contact is emphasized likewise by his intolerance for any kind of separateness, including those dictated by concerns over his safety or security. The pope refuses to ride in the bullet-proof Popemobile, and prefers instead riding in regular cars, such as the famous Fiat 500L in which he rode up to the White House, and he always gets out of the car to meet and hug people whenever he can. After the Solemn Inaugural Mass of the Pontificate on March 19, 2013, he surprised everyone by stopping his Jeep in St. Peter's Square to get out and hug a disabled person, and some months later, again during a crowded Wednesday in the Square, he embraced a man whose face had been disfigured by disease. Just as he has no fear of linguistic or communicative contamination, so as to reach the hearts and minds of people with vivid immediacy, so, too, Pope Francis has no fear of contamination or of the dangers around him in the physical world.

As for the virtual world, he remains similarly open, despite his protestations that the universe of technology is still somewhat beyond him. When asked about the practice of people wanting to take "selfies" with him, he said, "It's another culture. I feel like a great-grandfather! As I was leaving today, a policeman in his forties asked me for a selfie! I told him: you're a teenager! Yes, it's another culture but I respect it."[66]

His communicative acumen, which we have seen in so many situations, has allowed Pope Francis to read our present-day world correctly with all its new modalities of communication and its rapid expansion of horizons, limits, and media. Utterances that travel at the speed of a click or a tweet, brief collections of words that fly past our eyes every minute, every second, at our fingertips on our tablets and smart phones, are in the end still language and therefore allows for a dialogue between sender and receiver, as easily misunderstood, open to misinterpretation, corruption, and communicative confusion as any of these might be.

The new technologies of today represent a great resource for evangelization, and this is especially true for a missionary enterprise constantly on the lookout for even more suitable tools to reach people and entire populations hitherto inaccessible. And so it should be, because no means should go untried in order to bring the Word of God to all people. Thus, if one asks why, definitively, the Church and Christians ought to be online, the answer is simple: because the Church is called to be where the people are, and today, people live their lives online. As Benedict XVI observed, it's important to remember:

> Consecrated men and women working in the media have a special responsibility for opening the door to new forms of encounter, maintaining the quality of human interaction, and showing concern for individuals and their genuine spiritual needs. They can thus help the men and women of our digital age to sense the Lord's presence, to grow in expectation and hope, and to draw near to the Word of God which offers salvation and fosters an integral human development. In this way the Word can traverse the many crossroads created by the intersection of all the different "highways" that form "cyberspace," and show that God has his rightful place in every age, including our own." . . . This is one of the ways in which the Church is called to exercise a "diaconia of culture" on today's "digital continent." . . . Just as the prophet Isaiah envisioned a house of prayer for all peoples (see Isa 56:7), can we not see the web as also offering a

space—like the "Court of the Gentiles" of the Temple of Jerusalem—for those who have not yet come to know God?[67]

If Francis has an appreciation for social media, the Internet, too, has an appreciation for him, given that his name is one of the most frequently searched terms across search engines. His social networking pages are among the most followed, not merely because he is popular but because he has the capacity to shape opinion through his message, exponentially increasing its reach, showing himself to be much more effective than many who work to establish an online platform for themselves. His tweets and videos are not just passively viewed but create an ongoing exchange of views and opinions. This success is not just a matter of luck, but on the contrary, grows from a deep knowledge and awareness of the nature of these tools, which Bergoglio uses in a participatory way, not wishing to leave anyone out of the discussion and willing to listening to anyone and everyone, thereby turning online media into a space for sharing and conversation.

Pope Francis, however, is a long way from completely and uncritically accepting anything and everything that social media implies. He is not perfectly "integrated," as Umberto Eco's famous turn of phrase would have it.[68] Above all, he emphatically disagrees with the idea that the online world is enough and that virtual contact and conversation are sufficient for interaction between people. He insists that we stop and reflect, that we never set aside our relationship with reality, because the Gospel is born of reality. Only in an ongoing exchange with reality does the rapidity of social network interactions become a means for intentional action and not just idle chit-chat:

> May the light we bring to others not be the result of cosmetics or special effects but rather of our being loving and merciful "neighbors" to those wounded and left on the side of the road. Let us boldly become citizens of the digital world.[69]

Not just in how he acts but in the ways he relates to and speaks with others, Pope Francis has put himself at a great distance from the courtly ways and means of previous "imperial papacies." In his new paradigm, communication is not fashioned to flatter and seduce those listening; he doesn't conduct himself with an eye on the audience such that "the style with which the news is delivered ends up being more important that the news itself,"[70] which can lead to a variety of problematic outcomes. Rather, he raises up the deepest and most heartfelt questions of men and women and responds to them not with conceptual truisms but with experiential possibilities. For this reason, no subject is outside his area of concern, just as he does not have preconceived responses separate from the immediate, concrete relational context. His word bears witness and a passion, so that the Gospel becomes a word of newness, consolation, and salvation in all human affairs.

Pope Francis was able very quickly to see the dynamics of sharing and viralization inherent in digital media.[71] For Bergoglio, the Internet presents a great opportunity as a place to go out to the multitude on the existential margins of society who have need of light. In the virtual world, one can give someone a voice who has not had one, gain entry into social contexts that would otherwise be difficult or impossible to reach, to have an experience of the world and its suffering, and to respond to a call to be human:

> The digital world can be an environment rich in humanity; a network not of wires but of people. The impartiality of media is merely an appearance; only those who go out of themselves in their communication can become a true point of reference for others. Personal engagement is the basis of the trustworthiness of a communicator. Christian witness, thanks to the Internet, can thereby reach the peripheries of human existence.[72]

Provided, naturally, that our witness remains not just virtual nor merely verbal, for, as we have seen and will see, Pope Francis considers it fundamentally important that we go into the world, get our hands dirty, get involved in the simplest and yet most complex area of relationship, the encounter with other human beings:

> It is not enough to be passersby on the digital highways, simply "connected"; connections need to grow into true encounters. We cannot live apart, closed in on ourselves. We need to love and to be loved. We need tenderness. Media strategies do not ensure beauty, goodness, and truth in communication.[73]

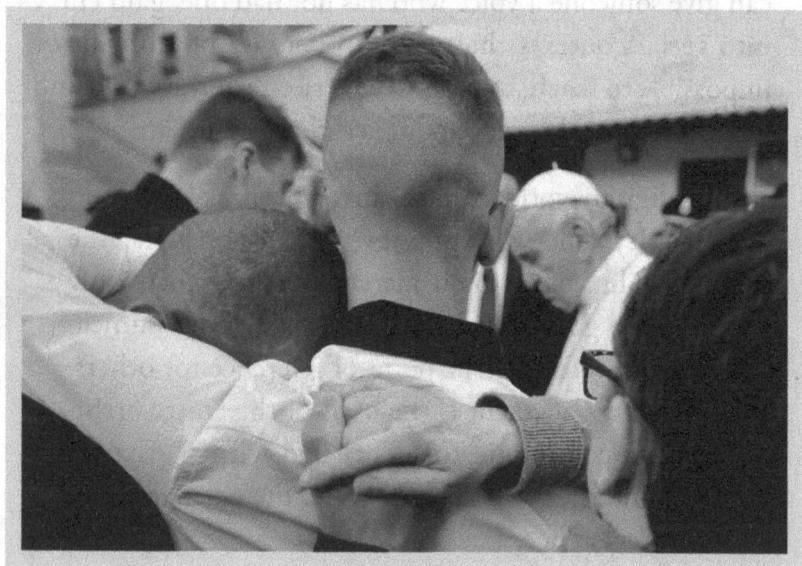

THREE

Encyclicals and Travels

> We must prepare ourselves for spiritual combat. . . . In
> this day and age unless Christians are revolutionaries
> they are not Christians. They must be revolutionaries
> through grace! Grace itself, which the Father gives us
> through the crucified, dead, and risen Jesus Christ.[1]

The Symbolic Function of Commitment on Major Issues

Our thinking nowadays, willingly or unwillingly,
is broadly dominated either by the impossibility,
brought to light at the end of the eighteenth century, of establishing a synthesis in representational
space or by the correlative obligation, simultaneously
occurring but instantly discordant, of opening up a
transcendental field of subjectivity and to fashion
thereby an encounter, beyond the object, with those
"near-transcendental" values that are for us Life,
Work, and Language.[2]

In this way, Foucault sums up a crucial but problematic
aspect of contemporary identity: what surrounds us is

all representation and narration, *métarécit*,[3] while at the same time what is meaningful to us exists *outside of ourselves*, something we must try to get close to by way of the dynamics of dialogue and encounter. On the one hand, we have a coherent, self-sufficient system of symbols, and on the other, an "objectivity" that is placed outside us: a connatural ambivalence in the human being's relationship to the world that in Pope Francis's actions is translated into a coherent union between his profession of faith and his concreteness of approach, which pays constant attention to real facts and the dynamics of history, politics, and society. This integration is one of those traits that Bergoglio owes to his Ignatian formation and which, right from the start, impelled him to take on issues of great social and global consequence: immigration, work, the environment, interreligious dialogue, inclusivity, poverty are all questions that he has never sidestepped and indeed have assumed a prominent place in his public statements.

He addresses such issues in the interview quoted earlier with Rádio Renascença, showing with his synthetic approach how none of them can be dealt with separately but instead need to be held as part of a complex, dysfunctional system:

> The immigration phenomenon is the tip of the iceberg. We see these refugees, these poor people fleeing war, fleeing hunger, but it's only the tip of the iceberg. Beneath it all there is a cause. And the cause is a wicked, unjust socio-economic system, because at the

center of an economic system, at the center of all of it, at the center of the world, if we want to mention ecology, at the center of a socio-economic society, at the center of politics, at the center there must be always be human beings. And today's dominant economic system has displaced human beings from the center, and at the center of it all is the idol that it is fashionable to worship these days, the god of money.

Where the cause is hunger, we must create sources for work and investment. Where the cause is war, we must seek peace, we must work toward peace. Nowadays the world is at war, at war with itself, or, as I say it, the world is in war by episodes, a piecemeal war, but it is also at war with the earth, because it is destroying the earth, our common home, the environment in which we live.[4]

Constantly present through all of Bergoglio's public statements and daily meditations, such matters are treated systematically and comprehensively in the encyclical letter *Laudato si'*, published in May 2015, and they become the heart of the speeches the pontiff makes during his apostolic visits during the summer of his third year to Ecuador, Bolivia, and Paraguay in July of that year and later to Cuba and the United States that September.

His addresses in North America assume a particularly important historical value. In the greeting he offered to President Barack Obama in the White House, for example, Francis mentions immigrants and witnesses to be a part of his own family's history:

As the son of an immigrant family, I am happy to be a guest in this country, which was largely built by such families. . . . American Catholics are committed to building a society that is truly tolerant and inclusive, to safeguarding the rights of individuals and communities, and to rejecting every form of unjust discrimination.[5]

After these preliminary remarks, however, the pope moves on to another matter of special personal importance to him, the environmental crisis, and he does so by quoting directly from his encyclical:

. . . climate change is a problem that can no longer be left to a future generation. When it comes to the care of our "common home," we are living at a critical moment of history. We still have time to make the changes needed to bring about "a sustainable and integral development, for we know that things can change" (*Laudato si'*, 13). Such change demands on our part a serious and responsible recognition not only of the kind of world we may be leaving to our children, but also to the millions of people living under a system that has overlooked them. Our common home has been part of this group of the excluded which cries out to heaven and which today powerfully strikes our homes, our cities, and our societies. To use a telling phrase of the Reverend Martin Luther King, we can say that we have defaulted on a promissory note and now is the time to honor it.[6]

In this statement, we note the abundance of terms drawn from the semantics of habitation: the nation "built" by "families," our "common home," the references to "children," and "knocking on our doors." While dealing with a multifaceted and complex subject, his speech is grounded in an image that is a concrete and everyday reality for us, our home. As we will see in this chapter, such is one of the basic characteristics of Bergoglio's "official" public discourse as laid out in the encyclicals and made manifest during his official visits. Pope Francis understands quite well that, just as language is symbol, so, too, is work a symbol, as is wealth, the environment, any shared human resource. His choice of major issues and how he addresses them is, before all else, a matter of *framing*: the context in which they will be presented (whether geographic or editorial) will determine their power as linguistic acts, and their symbolic frame of reference will shape the narrative and its public reception, which, from Rome to Quito, from Havana to New York, are rich with cultural interpretations, ideological significance, and diverse political agendas.

During his visit to the United States, Francis spoke to Congress, another choice with profound symbolic impact: standing in the heart of the nation's power, he made requests on behalf of those without political power, those unrepresented, the poorest of the poor, those abandoned by society. At the center of the nation's symbol of citizenship, he gives voice to those without citizenship. Thus, beyond the force of his words per se, it was this powerful choice of context that resulted in his speech having such a deep emotional effect on many of those listening (among whom John Boehner, Speaker of the House of Representatives, seen behind him with his eyes full of tears), as Francis was repeatedly interrupted by standing ovations from those in the balcony.

Bergoglio mentions Martin Luther King and the struggle for civil rights. But the most important place of his address to Congress—and his most pointed words—he reserves for the question of world peace, because the true victims of war are the poorest:

> Being at the service of dialogue and peace also means being truly determined to minimize and, in the long term, to end the many armed conflicts throughout our world. Here we have to ask ourselves: Why are deadly weapons being sold to those who plan to inflict untold suffering on individuals and society? Sadly, the answer, as we all know, is simply for money: money that is drenched in blood, often innocent blood. In the face of this shameful and culpable silence, it is our duty to confront the problem and to stop the arms trade.[7]

The power of Pope Francis's words, as we will see in the next section devoted to his apostolic visits, always depends on the context in which he speaks, and on the above question he will express himself even more forcefully after the terrorist attacks of November 13, 2015, in Paris, both at the Angelus on the Sunday after and in a homily a week after the tragic events:

Once, the pope recalled, Jesus said: "no one can serve
two masters: either God or wealth." And, he continued, "war is choosing wealth: 'let's make weapons,
this way the economy will balance out somewhat,'
and we continue with our interests." ... There is a hor-
rible word of the Lord: "accursed," because he said:
"blessed are the peacemakers!" So those who work
for war, who wage wars, are accursed, they are crimi-
nals. A war, the pontiff explained, "can be justified—
in quotation marks—with many, many reasons. But
when the whole world, as it is today, is at war—the
whole world!—it is a world war being fought piecemeal: here, there, there, everywhere." And "there is
no justification. God weeps. Jesus weeps."[8]

These words echo his speech given only months before to
the U.S. Congress and sum up the condemnation he casts
upon any "warmongers."

The trip to the United States, nevertheless, constitutes
a crucial moment in another way as well, which brings us
back to Bergoglio's life story. With his trip to the United
States, he concluded an itinerary that intentionally began
in South America (Ecuador, Bolivia, and Paraguay) and
then passed through Cuba, a visit of particular symbolic
value. Throughout its history, in fact, that island has always
been a hinge of sorts, a bridge between the North and the
South of the American continent, which is where, after all,
this pope comes from, and for the first time in the history
of the Church. If Karol Wojtyła was the first non-Italian

elected pope in five centuries, then Bergoglio is the first from a non-European nation and indeed, from literally the other side of the planet, from "the ends of the earth," as a matter of fact, as he put it when introducing himself.

Simplicity and Inclusion: The Apostolic Visits

All popes travel, but in Pope Francis's case, every trip is undertaken with an ear lent to his particular style of communication—simple, open, and keenly aware of the symbolism in word and context. The act of traveling itself, on its own, has a rich symbolic significance, reflecting the journey human beings endlessly undertake throughout the archipelago of our own finitude, or even more profoundly, as an image of the Divine as it passes uniquely from its own dimension of experience into our human history. By traveling, we meet ourselves and others, and at the same time, we meet our God who always goes before us, accompanying us, bringing together ultimately in himself all the diverse and broken paths we have trodden.

The particular ecumenical flavor of Francis's travels is one thing more this pontiff shares in common with St. Francis, who, during the time of the Fifth Crusade, from 1217 to 1221, took to the road to journey hundreds of miles, by land and by sea, for a conversation face-to-face with the then sultan of Egypt, Al-Malik al-Kamil, in the city of Damietta, outside of Cairo, which was the principal target of that crusade. Taking Cairo would have meant having control of the Nile River, and thus, all of Egypt, which would then be used as a staging area for the eventual invasion and conquest of Palestine. As the brother of Saladin, that warrior who above all others had come to symbolize Muslim resistance to the Crusaders, Al-Malik al-Kamal was entrusted with the defense of that city, which is why St. Francis came to him in an attempt to dissuade him from engaging in further warfare by converting him to a way of peace.

Saint Francis undertook this meeting under the rubric of dialogue, openness, and encounter: he was not there to debate the intellectual, theological, or political conflicts of that era, but rather he came to listen and to converse across their differing religious sensibilities. To his contemporaries, such an approach, beyond simply being dangerous, was scarcely comprehensible, and since the outcome of it was neither conversion nor surrender, ultimately his initiative was considered a failure. On the other hand, this communicative act, whereby St. Francis encouraged an encounter between the Gospel and the Qur'an, demonstrated even back then that intercultural communication and interreligious dialogue were possible, the same sort of communication and dialogue that John Paul II arranged for in 1986 in organizing the important interreligious encounter that occurred that year in Assisi.

Pope Bergoglio, too, has dedicated himself to the cause of interreligious dialogue and peacemaking, sharing with the holy man from Assisi that Christocentric vision which is key in understanding this pope's action, as Protestant biblical scholar Marcelo Figueroa suggests about his longtime friend Francis:

If we do not take into account the pages on which the Gospels are written, we will never understand him adequately. They are the source of his very particular way of communicating. The encyclicals, the homilies, his public speeches, his gestures, his lifestyle, and above all his deepest thoughts are all rooted in those pages. . . . Jesus dared to cross borders with surprising freedom and spontaneity. And he did this as a way to honor the first commandment to love God and one's neighbor. He had the courage to touch lepers and even the coffin of the dead son of the widow of Nain; he let the crowd press in around him, and in their midst he cured a woman considered unclean who was suffering from a disease. In concrete examples of encounter between differing faiths, he publicly acknowledged the faith of a Syro-Phoenician woman and had a lively theological conversation with a Samaritan woman as well. Thus, we understand why Francis, in the name of this Christocentric love, breaches security protocol so as to draw near to those who suffer. One can only conclude that mercy has been, right from the start, the most important of words for him, whose meaning and significance he learned and internalized from these politically incorrect gestures of the Messiah, Should we not think that his insistent encounters with people of other religions, especially those born of Abraham's line, are indeed the correct interpretation of a pure Christological mission?[9]

This is the lens through which we must read his various outreach initiatives, such the visit to the Rome Synagogue in January 2016, and even more, his apostolic visit to the Holy Land in 2014, some fifty years after Pope Paul VI's historic trip there to meet with Patriarch Athenagoras. Arising from a desire to promote dialogue within this troubled area of the world, he took advantage of the perfect occasion a few weeks later in the Vatican, praying together with Israeli president Shimon Peres and Palestinian president Mahmoud Abbas, as well as with Patriarch Bartholomaios. On that occasion, Francis made it a point to say:

I am profoundly grateful to you for accepting my invitation to come here and to join in imploring from God the gift of peace. It is my hope that this meeting will be a path to seeking the things that unite, so as to overcome the things that divide. Your presence, dear presidents, is a great sign of brotherhood which you offer as children of Abraham. It is also a concrete expression of trust in God, the Lord of history, who today looks on all of us as brothers and who desires to guide us in his ways. This meeting of prayer for peace in the Holy Land, in the Middle East, and in the entire world is accompanied by the prayers of countless people of different cultures, nations, languages and religions: they have prayed for this meeting and even now they are united with us in the same supplication. It is a meeting that responds to the fervent desire of all who long for peace and dream of a world in which men and women can live as brothers and sisters and no longer as adversaries and enemies.[10]

In every situation, Bergoglio delivers a message of peace, another characteristic he has in common with the holy man of Assisi and which perhaps, because of how he understands the life of this saint, seems to have become more and more prominent over time, as compared with other themes he addresses in his mission:

> Many people, when they think of Saint Francis, think of peace; very few people, however, go deeper. What is the peace that Francis received, experienced, and lived, and which he passes on to us? It is the peace of Christ, which is born of the greatest love of all, the love of the cross. It is the peace that the Risen Jesus gave to his disciples when he stood in their midst (see John 20:19-20).[11]

For St. Francis, as for Bergoglio, the call to Jesus remains the call to a participation in human suffering expressed through torment on the cross; thus, the cross becomes the symbol of Christianity, capable to communicating the power of God's merciful gaze upon us.

In visiting Assisi in 2013, he spoke of the relationship between St. Francis and the figure of Jesus:

> Where did Francis's journey to Christ begin? It began with *the gaze of the crucified Jesus*. With letting Jesus

look at us at the very moment that he gives his life for us and draws us to himself. Francis experienced this in a special way in the Church of San Damiano, as he prayed before the cross, which I too will have an opportunity to venerate. On that cross, Jesus is depicted not as dead but alive! Blood is flowing from his wounded hands, feet, and side, but that blood speaks of life. Jesus' eyes are not closed but open, wide open: he looks at us in a way that touches our hearts. The cross does not speak to us about defeat and failure; paradoxically, it speaks to us about a death that is life, a death that gives life, for it speaks to us of love, the love of God incarnate, a love that does not die but triumphs over evil and death. When we let the crucified Jesus gaze upon us, we are re-created, we become "a new creation." Everything else starts with this: the experience of transforming grace, the experience of being loved for no merits of our own, in spite of our being sinners. That is why Saint Francis could say with Saint Paul: "Far be it for me to glory except in the cross of our Lord Jesus Christ" (Gal 6:14).[12]

We should not be surprised, therefore, that one of Pope Francis's most important statements, the encyclical in which he addresses those themes dearest to his soul, suffused with a decidedly evangelical tone on issues ranging from the war against poverty to environmental protection, should find in St. Francis its explicit and principal inspiration.

Laudato si': An Encyclical of Poetry and Admonishment

Pope Francis's second encyclical letter is without a doubt the most discussed text of his pontificate thus far, since in it he firmly addresses the problem of "social ecology" within the modern world. By shining a light on the question of the relationship between society and environment, which is pastoral rather than scientific, it immediately became a worldwide topic of discussion.

It is clear, however, that the encyclical, starting with its title, is to be addressing its subject in unusual terms, with the intention of broadening and reorienting the ordinary ways we usually go about discussing the ever more urgent and unsolved issues we are facing with regard to social injustice and the environment. The encyclical's title is drawn from St. Francis's *Cantico delle creature*, the oldest poem in Italian literature, which is a straightforward hymn of praise to God, dense with imagery of life and nature, meditation and narrative. The saint from Assisi writes a poem brimming with a vision of the goodness of nature in which the image of the Divine can be seen through his creation, from which arises a familial relationship between human beings and the world around us. Before crying out against what does not work, therefore, Pope Francis's encyclical is a song of gratitude for all that is beautiful and good around us: a rhetorical strategy as indubitably effective as it is original. After all, what would focusing on ugliness and danger produce other than merely alienation and discouragement? By going about it from the other direction instead, focusing on the beauty of creation, he shows us first what must be defended and why. Our duty to undertake the preservation of creation is not assumed here but rather argued, and his choice of approach thereby guarantees that his affirmation will have more of an impact than any denunciation would have.

Making full use of the language and imagery of St. Francis, patron of the poor, brother to all, is another forceful rhetorical choice on the pope's part: we must not merely undertake the preservation of our environment, but we must all do so *together*. The Franciscan symbolic frame translates the necessity of being part of a whole human family—a revolution begun with the holy man of Assisi—into modern-day terms. Continuing all the great work done throughout the twentieth century by the Church and his predecessors to foster a better relationship between humanity and creation, Pope Francis emphasizes that "we need a conversation that includes everyone, since the environmental challenge we are undergoing, and its human roots, concern and affect us all."[13]

With *Laudato si'*, Pope Francis directs a call of inclusivity to everyone sharing our common home, believers, nonbelievers, and those professing other religious faiths. As Carlo Petrini, president and founder of Slow Food, also emphasized:

Holy Father Francis ... claims to have engaged in "reflections both joyous and dramatic." But I feel myself that the joy will prevail—and here I speak as a nonbelieving reader—though the presuppositions are deeply painful. It is the joy of being able to believe in revolutionary change and in a new humanity. . . . Francis addresses all people, as did John XXIII in *Pacem in terris* in 1963, which was dedicated to "all men of good will." It is a strong call to dialogue between religious faiths, between science and religion, between technological (and technocratic) areas of knowledge and ancient wisdom, between paradigms of understanding and all human beings. No one should be excluded.[14]

The worldwide press recognized the universal importance of Francis's message. "Pope Francis's encyclical on climate change, *Laudato si'*, is the most astonishing and perhaps the most ambitious papal document of the past 100 years, since it is addressed not just to Catholics, or Christians, but to everyone on earth."[15]

Under this sign of a universal human family, we are asked to explore the values at the core of our life together in society: "What is the purpose of our life in this world? Why are we here? What is the goal of our work and all our efforts? What need does the earth have of us?"[16]—not secondary concerns but fundamental questions. Here we stand at the place where our reflections and our exploration of reality intersect: to question the meaning behind our earthly actions is for Pope Francis not mere idle speculation but the very foundation for building a new society and is necessary if we are to live out the virtues of thoughtfulness and sharing in new ways. We find ourselves living on a planet being torn down by human carelessness, born of geopolitical and economic choices that are slowly destroying it and are creating an ever-widening gap between rich and poor. This gap must be healed, and the first action that needs to be undertaken is to listen to the poorest among us and to those who need "care."

Pope Francis, as we saw in the previous chapter, right from the start established the basis for an ongoing dialogue with those whom the world has forgotten, inviting all those listening to him to listen to them as well: individuals, families, local collectives, nation, the international community, in addition to, naturally, the Church. In *Laudato si'*, the pontiff gives official expression to the common thread running throughout the unbroken conversation *with* and *about* the poor, ensconcing it within the broadest possible invitation to an "ecological conversion," a phrase also used by John Paul II. The metaphor here, once again, is "care for our common home":

> We see increasing sensitivity to the environment and the need to protect nature, along with a growing concern, both genuine and distressing, for what is happening to our planet.... Humanity still has the ability to work together in building our common home.... men and women are still capable of intervening positively. Yet all is not lost. Human beings, while capable of the worst, are also capable of rising above themselves, choosing again what is good, and making a new start.[17]

Enzo Bianchi notes that in *Laudato si'*:

Pope Francis maintains the same style of writing and the same variety of tones and references that characterized his exhortation *Evangelii gaudium*. Thus, wanting to emphasize how everyone's identity is connected to the natural context in which we have lived and continue to live, he does not just remind that "soil, water, mountains: everything is, as it were, a caress of God" (*Laudato si'* 84), but he goes even further back to even more personal memories that each one of us shares, "Anyone who has grown up in the hills or used to sit by the spring to drink, or played outdoors in the neighborhood square; going back to these places is a chance to recover something of their true selves" (ibid.). Indeed, the "universal communion" that surrounds us is not an undifferentiated morass but rather a fabric of relationships, memories, stories, passion, and solidarity which embraces not just human beings but the whole of creation itself: "Everything is related, and we human beings are united as brothers and sisters on a wonderful pilgrimage, woven together by the love God has for each of his creatures and which also unites us in fond affection with brother sun, sister moon, brother river and mother earth (ibid. 92).[18]

This is not a statement of faith: our common home is not a place of worship, but rather a place of life, relationships, and sharing. Just as the environmental crisis affects every-

one, so, too, must the call to action around it be addressed
to everyone, and Pope Francis, in his writing here, adopts
the most inclusive strategy possible: "Rather than a problem to be solved, the world is a joyful mystery to be con-
templated with gladness and praise. All of us can cooper-
ate as instruments of God for the care of creation, each
according to his or her own culture, experience, involve-
ments, and talents."[19]

It is sufficient, moreover, to explore from the first chapter
the points he makes that will be dealt with throughout the
document: pollution and climate change, the issue of water
and the wars being fought over it, the decrease in biodiver-
sity and the deterioration of our quality of life due to social
decline, global sin, and the challenge of diversity. He does
not simply take up hot-button issues of contemporary dis-
cussions but also and above all traces those fault lines running across the entire planet which divide us and threaten to
tear us apart: "Change is something desirable, yet it becomes
a source of anxiety when it causes harm to the world and to
the quality of life of much of humanity,"[20] which requires
that we maintain a thought toward hope as well.

This choice of subject for an encyclical quickly drew a
great deal of interest, insofar as it sketched out a new spiritual perspective on the ever-increasing devastation wrought
by climate change, on the one hand, and the fate of the poor
who are the first victims of this devastation, on the other:

The dilemma between nature and person, before
which the encyclical places itself: take up the posi-

tion of *Shallow Ecology* in order to safeguard the primacy of the person . . . or affirm the thesis of *Deep Ecology*, with its risk of legitimizing a form of biocentrism that leaves no room for anthropology.... The basic framework of *Laudato si'* avoids this false dichotomy without adopting an attitude of cautionary prudence nor "becoming defensive." On the contrary, Pope Francis puts forward his thoughts in a radical way and does a two-step: on nature's side, he acknowledges its basic requirements, which call forth a global and integrated approach without settling for merely regional interventions; and on the other side, Pope Francis is quite explicit: "there can be no ecology without an adequate anthropology" (*Laudato si'* 118).[21]

His argument thus has a stunning clarity to it: attention to the suffering of the poor is not a question of charity but is about the survival of the planet. Once more, turning away from the usual rhetoric and changing up the perspective so as to present the issue in a different light, Pope Francis gave new life to a debate that has dragged on now for some time in a variety of ideologically sterile directions.

The *New York Times* in a long editorial underscores this particularly crucial passage in the text:

One remarkable aspect of the encyclical is that it focuses broadly on what he calls "the ecological crisis," and not just on a single aspect like pollution or global warming. The pope is concerned about all the ways humanity is damaging the planet, and how that environmental assault is returning like a boomerang to harm humanity itself.[22]

In the document we find repeated examples of this attention to the relationship between humanity and the planet, between humans and creation, between humans and nature, presented in all its myriad aspects with all their myriad consequences:

> the intimate relationship between the poor and the fragility of the planet, the conviction that everything in the world is connected, the critique of new paradigms and forms of power derived from technology, the call to seek other ways of understanding the economy and progress, the value proper to each creature, the human meaning of ecology, the need for forthright and honest debate, the serious responsibility of international and local policy, the throwaway culture and the proposal of a new lifestyle.[23]

The attention given to this encyclical was universal and across the board. Once again, Pope Francis was able to frame what is a common problem, the environmental crisis, its causes in social injustice and its effects on the survival of humanity, within a narrative and linguistic approach marked by *inclusion* rather than exclusion, by *dialogue* rather than ideological conflict. Bergoglio observes real life and asks questions, and, in the spirit of Ignatian discernment, asks questions of himself first and foremost, so as then to offer not just the answers but the very questions themselves in a spirit of openness to relationship and an endless, collective project of interpreting reality together.

In his writings, as in his personal communications, in short, Pope Francis "moves toward others." But to better understand the theological nature of this movement toward neighbor, we must take time to appreciate a notion that runs throughout his pastoral ministry: *Christian dynamism.*

A Church That Goes Forth

To fully grasp the concept of dynamism, we need to take into account the specific vision Bergoglio holds of how the Church should act and should live, which he views through a deeply Christocentric lens, which in turn was modeled on his personal experiences in Latin America wherein his faith took shape. Latin America Christianity has for a long time shown itself as having a deep connection to the everyday life of the people and which in its syncretism has no fear of contamination by symbols "outside" the faith but which rather grafts onto its own rituals all manner of creativity drawn from local cultures, such as songs, dance, and art. Because of its richness and realness, the Church is able to proclaim Christ with a special force to men and women assailed by the existential doubts and pains of day-to-day life in the modern world. As Pope Francis writes in *Evangelii gaudium,* "Jesus' whole life—his way of dealing with the poor, his actions, his integrity, his simple daily acts of generosity, and finally his complete self-giving—is precious and reveals the mystery of his divine life. Whenever we encounter this anew, we become convinced that it is exactly what others need."[24] Here is Jesus of the Gospels once more, among the people, who chooses his apostles from the people, the fishing boats, and the streets.

This Christocentric vision lifts up as significant our need to rediscover both a sense of urgency as well the joy that characterizes sharing the Word, promoting a so-called "new evangelization": this is the movement out of which Christian dynamism emerges. In part, this is a legacy Bergoglio receives from his predecessor, Benedict XVI; in the opening of his encyclical *Deus caritas est* Benedict writes that "being Christian is not the result of an ethical choice or a lofty idea, but the encounter with an event, a person, which gives life a new horizon and a decisive direction."[25] What is not envisioned here is some sort of contemplative cloistering in which one fashions for oneself a private and exclusive relationship with Jesus, but wholly the opposite: the compelling idea of a dynamic movement forward that carries the believer to a mature and fuller conception of the reality of the person of Christ and which therefore recognizes the transformative, indeed, revolutionary, power of the Gospel.

What is here envisioned, therefore, is a model of community in which a faithful expression of one's full humanity becomes a "quasi sacramental" revelation of the face of the Christ. There aren't two Churches—the Church of Christ and then a Church of human beings—but a single family of God in which the experience of history is an experience of grace, and vice versa. To teach this is not to teach one form of theology among many other possible theologies but is instead a lesson in that great manifestation of the Holy Spirit that—as we shall see in a bit—was the Second Vatican Ecumenical Council, especially as seen in its Constitutions *Lumen gentium* and *Gaudium et spes.*

A believer's lived experience requires from him or her a dynamic form of witness fitted to a social context not merely as an adaptation but one that makes of that social context the very foundation for the Church's example and practice in the real world. Through this lens, Bergoglio is quite specific when he says, "the Christian life isn't about standing in a corner calmly, carving out for oneself a comfortable path to heaven; it isn't sitting around in your living room,"[26] but the opposite: living one's Christianity has within it a dynamism that pushes one into the street, among the people, to discover the world. Pope Francis leaves nothing to chance and *humanity in particular is not left to chance.* Rather, he bears with us and listens to us. Christian life is realized in service carried out with apostolic zeal:

Not going forward to proselytize or rack up big numbers, in such and such a year there were that many more Christians who took these many more actions. Statistics are fine, they are helpful, but producing conversions isn't what God wants from us. What the Lord really wants from us is to proclaim reconciliation, that is the heart of his message: Christ became sin for me, and there sin is, in his body, in his soul. It's a crazy thing to say, but it is beautiful, because it is the truth. That's the scandal of the cross.[27]

We are with Jesus but we do not think like Jesus. We stay within our little groups but we lose our openness of heart, we lose our capacity for wonder, our gratitude and enthusiasm, and we risk "taking grace for granted." We may speak of Jesus and work for him, but still live far from his heart, which reaches out to those who are wounded. That is the temptation: living a "spiritual mirage," walking through the deserts of humanity without really seeing what's there, or indeed, only seeing what we want to see; we can create visions of the world but still not take in what the Lord puts right in front of our eyes. A faith that does not know how to take root in the life of real people remains arid, and instead of an oasis, produces more deserts.[28]

With Bergoglio, there is a change in direction, even an acceleration, in the push to carry the Gospel forward among the people that sets Church history apart by definition, which he himself defines as "the Church that goes forth." This dynamism, which we clearly see throughout Pope Francis's life history and religious formation, is the fruit of a long maturation process, and the narrative that characterizes his pontificate is the end point of a long journey rich with experiences lived out over many years. "In Revelation, Jesus says that he is standing at the threshold and calling. Evidently the text refers to the fact that he stands outside the door and knocks to enter. . . . But at times I think that Jesus may be knocking from the inside, that we may let him out."[29] In this image, one of the most striking of his pontificate (though still a cardinal at the time), we find all the fundamental elements of his symbolic world. The simplicity and uniqueness of the image give it a singular and immediate impact: the semantics of home, here not a caring refuge but a place where one can shut oneself in if one isn't open to the world; the concept of going forth, the necessity of movement:

> If a church, a parish, a diocese, an institution lives closed in upon itself, it grows sick. The same happens if you close yourself up in a room. And so, today we have a Church with rickets, with fixed rules, without creativity, full of certainty, or better said, sure of itself, an insurance company but without real safety. Instead, if one goes forth—a Church, a parish—goes forth to evangelize, what may happen is what happens to people who go out into the streets: you may have an accident. So, given the choice between a sick Church and a Church injured in an accident, I would prefer an injured Church that at least has ventured forth.[30]

In his apostolic exhortation *Evangelii gaudium*, we are invited "to go forth from our own comfort zone in order to reach all the 'peripheries' in need of the light of the Gospel,"[31] words that emphasize the need to see reality, to live it, to bend down and listen to it, because that is the only way to communicate the Gospel.

Besides, setting out on a journey, leaving behind a place of confinement, liberating oneself from slavery—literally as well as metaphorically—have been consistent themes at the heart of Christian tradition for a long time, and indeed, of the Old Testament before that. Every great change followed—or created—a pathway forward and out of a situation that was seen as oppressive or no longer tolerable. We think of Abraham leaving Haran for the land of Canaan; Moses on receiving the revelation atop Mt. Horeb and going forth to free the people of Israel from slavery; the travels of Jacob or, in a more figurative fashion, the vicissitudes of Job. But also, strikingly, the New Testament, likewise, as the apostles leave their homes and their former lives to follow Jesus.

As Pope Francis puts it, Christian will is always "the drive to go forth and give, to go out from ourselves, to keep pressing forward in our sowing of the good seed, and remains ever present."[32] It isn't an obligation but it's the force of a desire that grows out of the truth and one's decision to confront that truth, to enter into relationship with and grasp the full meaning of one's own faith. "It isn't simply a physical movement but participation in the very existence of Jesus, who went forth from the Father to live among us, without a place to lay his head, who was born and who died on the outskirts of the cities of Bethlehem and Jerusalem."[33]

As we saw in his thoughts on gift, Pope Francis sees this movement of the Church forward and out into the streets as very closely tied to his concept of a Church of the poor that has "nothing to lose" and everything to fear by hanging back: "When we forget this mission, forget about poverty, forget apostolic zeal and put our hope in these means, the Church slowly lapses into an NGO and becomes a fine organization: powerful but not evangelical, because that spirit is lacking, that poverty, that healing power."[34]

Here his communication, more than ever, takes on a substantial quality, for the moment that the Word of God is proclaimed *in* and *with* poverty, we become able to recognize our "neighbors" and relieve their misery:

> The Gospel should be proclaimed in poverty ... because salvation is not a theology of prosperity.... This is the mission of the Church: the Church which heals, which cures.... A few times I have spoken of the Church as a field hospital: it's true! How many wounded there are, how many wounded! How many people who need their wounds to be healed.... This is the Church's mission: healing the wounds of the heart, opening doors, liberating, and saying that God is good, that God forgives all, that God is Father, that God is gentle, that God always waits for us.[35]

Bergoglio's pastoral ministry therefore is carried out in a Church that turns back to its missionary direction, which is why his papacy is characterized by so much traveling and so many meetings: from his "outings" among the people of Rome to tend to the needs of the homeless or simply to meet people, up to and including the tremendous "mobs" that have gathered about him in various places of the world where, we have seen, symbols are being used to remind the faithful of their sacred obligation to witness to the faith.

Pope Francis brings words and light to these places, paying attention to all aspects of his communications, reaching across into the real world not just to share the Gospel but to bring these realities to the world as a whole, through continuous Christian dialogue, re-establishing the dignity and "sovereignty" of the people. He himself defines the theoretical terms of his action in this regard: "The ultimate aim should be that the Gospel, as preached in categories proper to each culture, will create a new synthesis with that particular culture."[36] In the words of theologian Marko Ivan Rupnik, "The point is that transmission of the faith means transmitting communion with God and participation in his life, along with the capacity to mold and shape one's mind and one's actions, that is, culture."[37]

Evangelii gaudium: Paths of the Church in the Future

With the election of Jorge Mario Bergoglio, one has the impression that a trajectory in the path of the earthly Church that opened with his predecessor popes of the twentieth century has now reached its high point. It began with the Second Vatican Ecumenical Council, which took on the task of designing a new Church capable of reaching out to the people rather than shutting itself up in the palaces of power. The first act of this Council, which puts itself forward as a specifically "pastoral constitution," was to build a bridge toward a rapidly changing society whose evolution, complexity, and doubts it felt the Church might not have adequately taken into account. "The joys and the hopes, the grief and the anxieties of the men of this age . . . are the joys and hopes, the grief and anxieties of the followers of Christ. Indeed, nothing genuinely human fails to raise an echo in their hearts."[38] It is the Church that opens itself up fully to the modern world.

With Pope Francis one has the sense that all these ideas have found their completion and fulfillment. The text in which this becomes immediately obvious is his first apostolic exhortation, entitled *Evangelii gaudium*, which focuses on the theme of proclaiming the Gospel in the world of today and which summarizes, among other things, the contributions of the Synod held in the Vatican from October 7 to October 28, 2012, on the theme "The New Evangelization for the Transmission of Christian Faith."

The words with which *Evangelii gaudium* begins are clear:

> The joy of the Gospel fills the hearts and lives of all who encounter Jesus. Those who accept his offer of salvation are set free from sin, sorrow, inner emptiness, and loneliness. With Christ joy is constantly born anew. In this exhortation I wish to encourage the Christian faithful to embark on a new chapter of evangelization marked by this joy, while pointing out new paths for the Church's journey in years to come.[39]

Contemporary people live in a state of isolation, which leads to closing oneself off from one's neighbor and to unhappiness in a vicious cycle of discouragement which feeds upon itself. This cycle can only be broken, argues the pope, by an encounter with Christ and with others through the sharing of the Gospel. We note right from the first pages of the exhortation that Bergoglio is strictly adhering to the use of a classic technique of argumentation: after a specific thesis (the invitation to undertake a "new chapter of evangelization") follows a step back for the presentation of the antithesis or problem (the loneliness of contemporary people) and then a leap forward with the proposal of a solution (Jesus)—a simple and effective technique that is a hallmark of this pope's approach to communication.

A Church whose sensibility is clearly pastoral is therefore the project that Pope Francis wishes to advance and to do so by basing it firmly within Christian tradition and translating it into the reality of today's world. The necessity he feels for accomplishing this comes alive through the pages of *Evangelii gaudium*, which are themselves born not only of his many travels and meetings during the first year of his pontificate but also spring from reflections on his life as a Christian. From the time he served as archbishop of Buenos Aires, in fact, he has dedicated himself to the mission of evangelization and community, and since that time, his objectives have not changed: building open communities of fellowship; the involvement of an active, aware laity; evangelization directed to all inhabitants of the city; aid to the poor and to the sick. To accomplish these objectives, he invites priests and laypeople to work together. Such actions are not the outcome of a

> sacrifice for its own sake nor some kind of obsession with austerity. It arises from stripping oneself down inwardly, not paying too much attention to oneself, so as to put God and others at the center of one's life. This has a pastoral significance, because it means being more available, nearer to the poor, to the limits of their social condition, to the humiliations they suffer. This is precisely why Bergoglio dislikes princely priests or "airport" bishops, ecclesiastic personages with golden cuff links, or those fond of their visits with the rich and powerful who constantly talk of themselves as superior to others.[40]

Pope Francis knows well that the transmission of the faith today is a complex question both theologically and pastorally, and he is determined to give new life to the deep sense of what it means to be pastoral, which he understands as the Church acting to foster encounter between human beings and the Gospel as incarnated within a specific historical-cultural context. As we have seen, all his communications have the aim of rooting a proclamation of the Gospel in the codes, contexts, and narratives of today's world. But all these actions move in the opposite direction as well: rendering the codes, context, and narratives of the Church transparent and comprehensible to the world, to society at large, and to "everyday people." The above represents one more example of his particular desire for openness and love of neighbor, which we explored earlier in this chapter.

It is in this sense that *Evangelii gaudium* represents a turning point wherein it is possible to glimpse, for the first time in an official text, his hermeneutic and communicative intention. As we have said, the text makes use of various contributions from the work of the October 2012 Synod in order to make them accessible to everyone, having never been fully presented outside the synodical context from which they arose but only known in partial, piecemeal, or even distorted form (as would happen with the Synod on the Family in 2015, whose internal disagreements and tensions were exaggerated by the media in ways not entirely warranted). As such, the work of this synod would never have reached its full potential in illustrating and exemplifying the pastoral path as chosen by this pontiff, which is why Pope Francis sets about narrating the work of this synod and by way of this official text opens the doors of the synod to his readers. Thus, *Evangelii gaudium* becomes "text" in the original etymological sense of the term, "textured" or "woven," in which a pattern can be seen, with strands of Pope Francis's pastoral and spiritual memory interlaced with his vision of today's world, the "coming together" of the Church's work, and his exhortation to seize this moment of grace to undertake, with faith and conviction, a new chapter in the path of evangelization.[41]

The tap root of his writing is the rediscovery of a joy born from the heart of the resurrected Christ and which is the fruit of the Holy Spirit, that joy which for Bergoglio in large part corresponds to the Ignatian notion of spiritual consolation, "all interior joy that invites and attracts what is heavenly and for the salvation of one's soul by filling it with peace and quiet in its Creator and Lord."[42] Bergoglio underscores that "all have a right to receive the Gospel. Christians have the duty to proclaim the Gospel without excluding anyone. Instead of seeming to impose new obligations, they should appear as people who wish to share their joy, who point to a horizon of beauty and who invite others to a delicious banquet. It is not by proselytizing that the Church grows, but 'by attraction.'"[43]

The adjective "attractive," applied to preaching, pastoral ministry, ways of communicating faith, appears in the text around thirty times, and along with "joy" and "attraction" constitutes one of the key words that we have highlighted in the writings of Pope Francis: dialogue, care, dynamism, joy. The dimensions of the message when taken as a whole are very obvious, for the inclusion of the concepts of "rejoicing" and "joy" open the semantic field *upward,* one might say, explicitly weaving the divine into the relationship of dialogue and care, giving it the role of guide in developing that dynamic movement of openness and evangelization. We are in relationship with others because we are in relationship with God; we are capable of care and mercy because we are beloved of God; we are able to go toward our neighbors because we come from God and to God we return. The joy and the force of attraction of which *Evangelii gaudium* speaks become the conceptual framework within which all the social and communicative action proposed by Pope Francis takes place and becomes possible.

In what seems initially like a paradox, we might therefore say that beneath any communication there lies a "good" that does need to be communicated but which communicates itself as the son of that singular communicative act par excellence, namely, Jesus Christ, the person in whom Word and gift are united in the ultimate union of witness and sacrifice.

> Jesus can also break through the dull categories with which we would enclose him, and he constantly amazes us by his divine creativity. Whenever we make the effort to return to the source and to recover the original freshness of the Gospel, new avenues arise, new paths of creativity open up, with different forms of expression, more eloquent signs and words with new meaning for today's world. Every form of authentic evangelization is always "new." [44]

This newness sweeps away any prophetic obscurity and expresses itself with that narrative immediacy that gives life to the whole New Testament, an extraordinary narrative full of stories, figures, explanations that the heart and minds of even humble people can grasp, and yet dense with challenging truths. In the face of this proposition, "the papacy and the central structures of the universal Church also need to hear the call to pastoral conversion,"[45] Bergoglio admonishes in the exhortation. This conversion would translate Gospel language into today's categories of thought such that the Church's thoughts and directions are made accessible and comprehensible to the people, bringing a Christocentric and Christological vision into narrative action as an act of language and an act of caring.

Precisely because of this need for cohesiveness and focus in the message, Pope Francis "asks that less emphasis be placed on secondary questions but that the proclamation concentrate instead on what is essential, that there be a proper balance, and that things are placed in the proper context."[46] He is very aware that nowadays, as in the classical era, language "is a prisoner in the latticework of thought and woven in the very web in which this latter occurs. It is not an external effect of thought, but is itself thought. . . . Representation, occurring in the verbal signs that manifest it, becomes *discourse*." [47] And discourse, we might add, becomes the reality of change and of a palingenesis, a renewal that is the broadest horizon of Pope Francis's mission.

Joy to the Farthest Reaches of the World

"Gospel" is a term that etymologically implies the need for proclamation—from the Latin *evangelium*, which is in turn derived from the Greek εὐαγγέλιον, composed of εὐ, "well, good," and ἄγγελος, "messenger, announcement." It literally means "good news." To evangelize thus signifies for Bergoglio bringing a message of joy to the most remote corners of the world. Indeed, in the preceding paragraphs we have examined just how in the official texts of his pontificate there is woven together significant theological and philosophical thought that stands behind the force with which he takes on some of the most crucial questions of our time. But one of the most significant places of Pope Francis's communicative action is the moment when reflection and intention make themselves physically known in movement, in a word, traveling.

Traveling, in Latin *viaticum*, that is, the provisions necessary in order to undertake a journey, becomes immediately part of evangelization in Christian tradition. Jesus is always on the road, and his *viaticum* is the word of God that becomes a reality. Thus, it was also for St. Francis of Assisi, who took to the road with a spiritual urgency to bear witness that Jesus himself walked among human beings and proclaimed the Word. More generally, the experience of "traveling" belongs to all of us, whether as a journey or a discovery, exploration, or pilgrimage. It is, therefore, a potent metaphor and at the same time inclusive, bringing together believer and nonbeliever, which is precisely why it is necessary.

Indeed, why else would a papal trip be necessary, what with all its logistical complexities and, of course, not without its dangers? Why necessary at all, one might ask, especially these days in an age of global communication in which any one of us can send pictures to the far reaches of the planet? And yet, the need to proclaim the Gospel among the people has meant for many popes physically going on the road to journey about the world, and Bergoglio, too, has made traveling one of the key pieces of pastoral ministry. Right from the start, he moved among the people, riding in small and very ordinary cars. One of the symbols he uses to illustrate the desirability of a simple life is his overnight bag in which he carries his personal effects and books, like any other commuter in the world. And even while traveling, he made clear right away he would do away with security oversight or limits on his person or oversight so as to allow the essentials of his presence and proclamation to emerge freely. In terms of communication, we might say that he sought to eliminate as much as possible any "background noise" that might block or distort what he had to say being heard accurately and completely.

By placing Pope Francis's travels within the framework of his overall communicative action, we must keep in mind the narrative function of space.

> Space takes on meaning insofar as, within it, are shaped a series of actions that live it and pass through it. This series of actions forms a *narrative*, for a number of reasons: (i) because these actions are not organized randomly but are meaningful since they are articulated in view of programs of greater or less complexity; if spaces are functional for someone, they are not merely so in the sense of banal instrumentality, but because they stimulate (or impede) determined forms of behavior; (ii) because as over against one subjectivity's program of action is opposed the program of another's subjectivity; so if a certain space takes on meaning it does so because a polemical narrative, with a series of strategies and intersubjective tactics, is shaped within it; (iii) finally, because neither actions nor intersubjective relationships are shaped within the space in the sense that certain

spaces provoke certain behavior but rather because, more deeply, they make place for subjects and thus take upon themselves human action, making them their own; spatial organizations carry out actions in the place of human beings.[48]

In this sense, Bergoglio's traveling is the opportunity to display *real* tensions, the fault lines of politics and society, in a *narrative* fashion, to show where they are and then to resolve them, using as a "curative principle" the symbolic power of ritual, gesture, and presence.

So with this, we close the circle and arrive back to where we started with that first "Good evening" from the Balcony of Blessing on St. Peter's Square, in his first public appearance, understandable now as a right and proper ceremony of transformation. Even a papal trip is a communicative act with considerable hermeneutic force, because, in contemporary terms, it "makes news," and therefore it directs the agenda of the media by offering a global platform for the message, focusing the attention and, in the best of cases, the intention of Christian peoples all over the planet. Let us not forget in fact that, as results of research on the effect of television news on the public have shown, there is a strong correlation between the agenda set by the media and the perception of the problem in public opinion. "Information delivered by the media constitutes, for many people, their only contact with politics. . . . On every subject, many 'hear' but few 'listen,'"[49] and the best way to get them to listen is to focus the most media attention possible on the subject and to make the message as simple as possible. Pope Francis has shown himself to be a master at both of these things.

How can one forget Lampedusa, his first official visit in Italy, on July 8, 2013? Upon his arrival on the island, he met with a group of undocumented migrants and refugees, after which, in a boat accompanied by fishermen—a choice, we should note, that is both practical and rich with New Testament symbolism—he threw a crown of flowers into the sea over the point where, fifty yards down, a statue of the Madonna of the Sea had been placed in memory of those who had lost their lives in crossing the channel to Sicily. His homily that day is among the most powerful and moving so far in his entire pontificate:

> a sense of responsibility for our brothers and sisters . . .
> we see our brother half dead on the side of the road,
> and perhaps we say to ourselves: "poor soul . . . !," and
> then go on our way. It's not our responsibility, and
> with that we feel reassured, assuaged. The culture
> of comfort, which makes us think only of ourselves,
> makes us insensitive to the cries of other people,
> makes us live in soap bubbles which, however lovely,
> are insubstantial; they offer a fleeting and empty illu-
> sion which results in indifference to others; indeed,
> it even leads to the globalization of indifference. . . .
> Has any one of us wept because of this situation and
> others like it? Has any one of us grieved for the death
> of these brothers and sisters? Has any one of us wept
> for these persons who were on the boat? For the

young mothers carrying their babies? For these men who were looking for a means of supporting their families? We are a society that has forgotten how to weep, how to experience compassion—"suffering with" others: the globalization of indifference has taken from us the ability to weep! . . . Has anyone wept? Today has anyone wept in our world?[50]

We see here the repeated use of the interrogative, which goes beyond a mere rhetorical device and directly addresses the listeners there, "calling" them to his words, bringing them into a *relationship of presence* with the victims and the human tragedy they suffered, lending great power to a message already grounded within a powerful communicative context.

Likewise, Bergoglio's second official visit within Italy marks an important stage in his development of a coherent and functional communicative framework. In Cagliari on September 22, 2013, the pope met with individuals from the world of business and commerce along with a number of workers, many of whom were unemployed or had been laid off. On this occasion, as he would do more and more often in a symbolic gesture, he set aside his written remarks and spoke off the cuff:

There was no work! And in my childhood I heard talk of this period at home. . . . I never saw it, I had not yet been born, but I heard about this suffering at home, I heard talk of it. I know it well! However, I must say to you: "Courage!" Nevertheless I am also aware that for my own part I must do everything to ensure that this term "courage" is not a beautiful word spoken in passing! May it not be merely the smile of a courteous employee, a Church employee who comes and says "be brave!" No! I don't want this! I want courage to come from within me and to impel me to do everything as a pastor, as a man. We must all face this challenge with solidarity, among you—also among us—we must all face with solidarity and intelligence this historic struggle.[51]

We notice here an apparent contradiction: the spoken word, ephemeral by definition, is given more weight and considered more "solid" as compared to the written text. Why? Because according to what we might call his poetics, his dedication to acknowledging what is real at all times, the spoken word is rooted in a context; it "belongs" to the listeners in a relationship that is here and now.

And there is something else interesting in what he did in this speech: to set aside a written text to enter instead into a more immediate and authentic dialogue is to offer something freely and without price, a gratuitousness that fits perfectly with the message Pope Francis wished to communicate at that moment: the uncertainty of work has definite causes: "it is the result of a global decision, of an economic system that leads to this tragedy; an economic system centered on an idol called 'money.'" . . . Lord Jesus, you were never out of work, give us work and teach us to fight for work and bless us all. In the name of the Father, of the Son, and of the Holy Spirit."[52]

This theme of work has precedents in Pope Francis's statements, for example, the homily he gave at Santa Marta on one particular day, May 1, 2013: "dignity does not give us power, money, or culture. No! It is work that gives us dignity, but today so many social, political, and economic systems have made decisions that exploit people."[53]

In the Cagliari meeting, it is therefore clear that the trip and the meeting are the principal vehicles for the communication of a message that is grounded in the flesh and blood suffering of real people and which cannot be delegated to the abstract dimension—literally *mediated*—in, say, a television appearance. This dynamic can be seen in all his many international travels, which represent important stages in the progress of his pontificate. The first was Rio de Janeiro, in Brazil, on July 22, 2013, where he came to celebrate the 28th World Youth Day. To the young people there, Pope Francis launched a clear and concise appeal: "The Lord needs you, young people, for his Church. My friends, the Lord needs you! Today too, he is calling each of you to follow him in his Church and to be missionaries. . . . Please, don't leave it to others to be the protagonists of change. You are the ones who hold the future!"[54]

As usual, he does not forget to conclude his appeal with narrative precision, this time, focusing on the concept of time and stages of life:

But at the other end of life, the elderly, they too are the future of a people. A people has a future if it goes forward with both elements: with the young, who have the strength, and things move forward because they do the carrying; and with the elderly because they are the ones who give life's wisdom. And I have often thought that we do the elderly an injustice, we set them aside as if they had nothing to offer us; they have wisdom, life's wisdom, history's wisdom, the homeland's wisdom, the family's wisdom. And we need all this! That is why I say that I am going to meet the young, but within their social context, principally with the elderly.[55]

The path is clear: from the energy of youth, through the experiences of life, to the wisdom of old age, which in its turn nurtures the enthusiasm of youth. We see that the narrative arc here makes a hermeneutic circle: the experience of the world becomes *interpretation* of the world, and therefore, understanding, and even more, a capacity for relationship. Obviously, that the pope would engage in such a reflection in the midst of traveling, that is to say, in the middle of an experience, once again shows how closely tied together text and context are for what he means to say.

One trip of enormous symbolic value was his journey in September 2015 to both Cuba and the United States, an event that marked an important transition point in the history of the relationship between those two countries, which has, in recent years, warmed significantly. In fact, the flight that brought the pope from Santiago in Cuba to Washington, DC, the capital of the United States, was the first such flight in almost fifty years. This trip carried a message, and such a simple crossing was intended to connect two separate realities that had, for decades and decades, armed themselves against each other. The passage was tracked by radar, the small blip of the airplane as it made its way from one place to the other; here we see a bridge thrown across the ruins of history, a bridge built, no less, by a pope who had come "from the ends of the earth," which lends the event even further meaning: one must come forth, even out of the far corners of the earth, to give of oneself, to give the gift of a conversation that might truly unite continents, span oceans, lessen the distance between us:

> In an era of increasing conflict, the pope invites us to build bridges, "little bridges, but the smallest bridges" little by little, one after another "make one big bridge to peace." It's about "the ability to bring together," to create "social friendships" for the common good within the midst of diversity. "Our method," he stated, "is dialogue, not as clever strategy but from faithfulness to He who never tires" of putting forth "his invitation of love." We offer the treasure of the Gospel—that is his exhortation—with humility, setting aside "the harsh and warlike language of division": "only the lasting charm of kindness and love remain truly convincing." We also keep in mind that the other person is a "brother to be reached and redeemed." Concrete actions of this "bridge building" are the rapprochement between the United

States and Cuba and the announcement of the peace accord in Colombia, both thanks to Pope Francis, after a half century of fighting.[56]

In the American portion of his visit, Pope Francis does not miss the occasion to focus on the theme of freedom. Once again, he knows how to take advantage of the context and cultural codes to ground his remarks in the reality of the here and now and to make his inspiring and universal message understandable to all:

> Freedom and justice go together. These are the two words that the pope repeats in Cuba and in the United States. "A nation can be considered great when it defends freedom," promotes "full rights for everyone," "fights for justice and on behalf of the oppressed," "sows peace." The pope invokes "home, work, and land" for everyone, freedom of religion and of conscience, the right to life in all stages of development (no even to the death penalty), defense of the environment. In the face of the great challenge of immigration, he recalls the golden rule of the Gospel, "Do unto other as you would have them do unto you." He advocates for an end to the persecution of ethnic and religious minorities and to the arms trade.[57]

"A great heart, Jesus' heart": thus read one headline in a Korean newspaper.[58] That is how the pope and his travels to that country are remembered because of what he said and what he did. And sometimes what he says troubles the conscience, as in Daejon, in the fishbowl of the World Cup Stadium,[59] where he invited those listening to fight against "a fascination with materialism that suffocates authentic spiritual and cultural values and the spirit of frantic competition that fosters egotism and conflict . . . inhuman economic models that create new forms of poverty and sideline workers." In Seoul, in Gwanghwamun Plaza, during the beatification of 124 martyrs, before 8,000 of the faithful, he emphasized that their example teaches the importance of charity in the life of faith and that to be a martyr is to be above all a witness to Jesus. In the sanctuary of Haemi, his witness and his empathy toward young people touched the heart of children who had come there from all over that continent: "Rise up! You are the hope of Asia!" he said to them. In the Myeong-dong Cathedral, he emphasized that the gift of reconciliation, of unity, and of peace are inseparably linked to the grace of conversion and that the prophetic power of the cross of Christ overcomes all divisions, heals all wounds, and re-establishes the original bond of fellowship between people. Again, the choice of traveling by train (economy class), his visit to his fellow Jesuits at Sogang University, the baptism of one of the fathers of one of the victims of the Seoul ferry disaster, his smiles, his hugs, his selfies with young people, the ever-increasing time he took throughout for a word, a handshake, countless hugs given to even the smallest children in the crowd, all these took up pages and pages in the local newspaper. Thanks to Pope Francis, the eyes of the world were trained on Korea, "the land of the morning calm," which saw the nation without walls for the first time, speaking only one language, the language of peace and hope.

In sketching out this image of an "ideal geography" in which Pope Francis pursues his work of evangelization and communication, we cannot overlook his trip to Africa at the end of November 2015, which takes him to one of the most desperate and tormented realities on the planet: Kenya, Uganda, and the Central African Republic. Justifiable concerns for his safety—in the immediate aftermath of the November 13 terrorist attacks in Paris that year— did not lead the pope to foreswear his poetics of closeness, inclusion, and simplicity: he traveled in his Popemobile top down and walked among the crowds, as usual. For if a message is not consistent in all its parts, there is the risk that it will be ineffective, and this apostolic visit was charged with far too great a symbolic investment for him to risk missing the target.

It was precisely the last and most dangerous leg of his journey, his time in the Central African Republic, that Bergoglio chose for the most meaningful act of his trip: the opening of the first Holy Door, at the Cathedral of Bangui, the capital, which officially began the Extraordinary Jubilee Year of Mercy. In the history of the Church, and in world history, this is the first time that the first Holy Door was opened outside of Rome to officially begin the first "worldwide Jubilee" in human history, quickly rechristened a "Jubilee on the periphery," adopting that theme dear to the pope, reaching out to care for the least among us. The pope opens the Holy Door but not "to enter in" as much as "to go forth." And in this highly symbolic context, he chose to send a powerfully provocative message: open your arms to your enemies, as Jesus teaches. "I come as a pilgrim of peace and an apostle of hope,"[60] he announces. "To all those who make unjust use of the weapons of this world, I make this appeal: lay down these instruments of death! Arm yourselves instead with righteousness, with love and mercy, the authentic guarantors of peace."[61]

Even on this occasion, the pope's trip mirrors a symbolic pathway to a Gospel message: "love your neighbors and pray for those who persecute you" (Matthew 5:44); the reality of a country torn apart by war; the arms race and the escalation of conflict—urgent questions in a world hanging on the precipice of a world war. Text, context, and metatext, all offered to believers and nonbelievers alike, within a great collective ceremony broadcast worldwide which frames the narrative within symbolic gestures of historical importance, such as the opening of *that* Holy Door, the high point of a communicative intention built up over time so as to bring to all hearts and minds a singular message of salvation:

> Even when the powers of Hell are unleashed, Christians must rise to the summons, their heads held high, and be ready to brave blows in this battle over which God will have the last word. And that word will be one of love and peace![62]

CONCLUSION

The Revolution of Mercy

"We are living in a time of mercy." These are the words pronounced by Pope Francis after the Angelus of January 11, 2015. On December 8, the day after the opening of the Holy Door of the Basilica of St. Peter in Rome, he will say, "This Extraordinary Year is itself a gift of grace. To pass through the Holy Door means to rediscover the infinite mercy of the Father who welcomes everyone and goes out personally to encounter each of them. It is he who seeks us! It is he who comes to encounter us! This will be a year in which we grow ever more convinced of God's mercy."[1] Between these two statements, spoken almost a year apart, came his decision to announce an Extraordinary Jubilee.

With the ceremony of the opening of the first Holy Door in Rome, televised live throughout the world by the Vatican Television Center on the day the universal Church is celebrating the Feast of the Immaculate Conception, we can say that we have come full circle in our consideration of the Pope Francis's communications. Why at this point? Let us recall certain characteristics of this particular event.

First of all, the choice of date in initiating the Holy Year: December 8, Third Sunday of Advent, and Feast of the Immaculate Conception. A day laden with symbolism about waiting for grace, promise, welcome, gift—in short, the joyful universe of meanings that we have seen run through every level of this pope's messages. Thus declares the Bull of Indiction for the Extraordinary Jubilee:

> The Holy Year will open on December 8, 2015, the Solemnity of the Immaculate Conception. This liturgical feast day recalls God's action from the very beginning of the history of humanity. After the sin of Adam and Eve, God did not wish to leave humanity alone in the throes of evil. So he turned his gaze to Mary, holy and immaculate in love (see Eph 1:4), choosing her to be the mother of man's redeemer. When faced with the gravity of sin, God responds with the fullness of mercy. Mercy will always be greater than any sin, and no one can place limits on the love of God who is ever ready to forgive. I will have the joy of opening the Holy Door on the Solemnity of the Immaculate Conception. On that day, the Holy Door will become a *Door of Mercy* through which anyone who enters will experience the love of God, who consoles, pardons, and instills hope.[2]

Thus, we come to the second characteristic of the Jubilee, the opening of the numerous Holy Doors in Rome and throughout the world. The opening of the Holy Door is itself an ancient rite, performed for the first time in 1423 by Pope Martin V, who officiated at this rite in the Basilica of Saint John Lateran. Only at Christmas 1499, in fact, inaugurating the Holy Year that would begin the next century, did Pope Alexander VI put in practice the opening of the doors of the other Roman basilicas: St. Peter, St. Mary Major, and St. Paul outside the Walls. Indeed, it was on that occasion that the door was opened at the front of St. Peter that is still in use as the entrance today.

The first Holy Door opened by Pope Francis, however, was not that of a Roman basilica: the very first rite of opening, as we have seen, was on the continent of Africa, so as to put even more emphasis on its meaning, thus ensuring that it would be seen and reseen over and over, throughout the world, during the entire course of the ensuing year. Once again we read in the Bull of Indiction:

On the following Sunday, the Third Sunday of Advent, the Holy Door of the Cathedral of Rome—that is, the Basilica of Saint John Lateran—will be opened. In the following weeks, the Holy Doors of the other papal basilicas will be opened. On the same Sunday, I will announce that in every local church, at the cathedral—the mother church of the faithful in any particular area—or, alternatively, at the co-cathedral or another church of special significance, a Door of Mercy will be opened for the duration of the Holy Year. At the discretion of the local ordinary, a similar door may be opened at any shrine frequented by large groups of pilgrims, since visits to these holy sites are so often grace-filled moments, as people discover a path to conversion. Every Particular Church, therefore, will be directly involved in living out this

Holy Year as an extraordinary moment of grace and spiritual renewal. Thus, the Jubilee will be celebrated both in Rome and in the Particular Churches as a visible sign of the Church's universal communion.[3]

As was noted, here we have the first worldwide Jubilee in history, with many Holy Doors being opened all over the earth. The metaphor is clear and at the same wholly at one with Pope Francis's communicative actions. "Jesus is knocking to go out," and the Church throws itself wide open in the same way to create a pathway to grace for believer and nonbeliever. No one is excluded, even the excluded. Moreover, Pope Francis, ten days after opening the door of St. Peter's, likewise opens the Holy Door of charity at the Caritas Hostel, next to the Termini train station, a spot in the city's center rife with individuals on the margins of society. In response to such a gesture, as he himself says, the only answer can be as loving as God is himself:

> How much wrong we do to God and his grace when we speak of sins being punished by his judgment before we speak of their being forgiven by his mercy (see Saint Augustine, *De praedestinatione sanctorum*, 12, 24)! But that is the truth. We have to put mercy before judgment, and in any event God's judgment will always be in the light of his mercy.[4]

Mercy is a key word, not just for the Holy Year, but in Christian theology:

One cannot understand a true Christian who is not merciful, just as one cannot comprehend God without his mercy. This is the epitomizing word of the Gospel: mercy. It is the fundamental feature of the face of Christ: that face that we recognize in the various aspects of his existence—when he goes to meet everyone, when he heals the sick, when he sits at the table with sinners, and above all when, nailed to the cross, he forgives; there we see the face of divine mercy. Let us not be afraid; let us allow ourselves to be embraced by the mercy of God who awaits us and forgives all. Nothing is sweeter than his mercy. Let us allow ourselves to be caressed by God; the Lord is so good, and he forgives all.[5]

And this is the third characteristic: we have a widespread Jubilee in which is ensconced the *social* nature of this pontiff's communicative actions. It is not by chance that @Pontifex_it tweeted the following on December 8: "May the Jubilee of Mercy bring the kindness and tenderness of God to all!" Upon examination, we could similarly use the term *social network* with regard to the first Jubilee in the history of the Catholic Church, declared in the year 1300: Pope Boniface VIII was in some ways pushed toward announcing one under the pressure of numerous pilgrims who, starting the year before, in 1299, began to flow into the capital, because word had been spread that the pope would be extending a plenary indulgence in conjunction with the beginning of the century.

So, while it is true that all Jubilees entail wide participation on the part of the faithful, the inclusivity and the
engagement in dialogue that are "ground level" aspects
of Pope Francis's communications represent emphases
and directions without prior precedent and which turn
the occasion into an authentically collective rite for all, a
rite that continues and brings to fulfillment that mediat-
ing, transformative ceremony begun years before on the
Balcony of Blessing of St. Peter's, with a simple, weighty
"Good evening."

Continuity, thus, within change. A Jubilee is certainly
not a "revolutionary" act: it is a way to prepare for one, to
understand one, and to celebrate being one. But in what
way, exactly, can we speak of "revolution," communicative
or otherwise, with regard to this pope? From a doctrinal
point of view, in fact, Bergoglio is most certainly not revolutionary, which is one of those points of misunderstanding
that has arisen due to the extemporaneous nature of many
of his statements. As he explained himself with a story to
journalists on his flight from Cuba to the United States,

A friend of mine, a cardinal, told me about a lady
who came to him very concerned, a good Catholic
lady, a bit rigid but very good, and asked him if it
was true that the Bible talked about an antichrist.
He explained that it is found in the book of Revelation. Then she asked if it spoke of an antipope!
"Why do you ask?" he said. "Because I am sure that
Pope Francis is the antipope!" "And where did you

get that idea?" "Because he doesn't wear red shoes!" There it is, as it happened. The reasons for thinking that someone is a communist or not . . . I am sure that I haven't said anything more than what is contained in the Church's social teaching. On the other flight [returning from Latin America], one of your colleagues—I don't know if she is here—said, after I went to speak to the popular movements, "You held out a hand to this popular movement"—something more or less like that—"but will the Church follow you?" And my reply was: "I'm the one who follows the Church." I do not believe I was wrong there. I don't believe that I have said anything not found in the Church's social teaching. Things can be explained, and maybe an explanation could give the impression of being a little more "leftist," but that would be an error of explanation. No, my teaching, on all of this, in *Laudato si'*, on economic imperialism and all these things, is that of the Church's social teaching. And if I need to recite the Creed, I am ready to do it![6]

Church doctrine, in the end, is always what the Gospel teaches, and if Bergoglio manages to make it seem remarkable, that is because he has the capacity to dress it up narratively and make it effective by way of what we have termed his "linguistic actions." In that sense, for him, it is in change that true fidelity to Church teaching resides:

To stay faithful implies going forth. Indeed, to be with the Lord, one leaves oneself behind. Paradoxically, though, in staying faithful, by being faithful, one changes. One cannot stay faithful, like traditionalists or fundamentalists, by following the letter. Faithfulness is always to change, to blossom, to grow.[7]

It would therefore be cheap and easy to reduce Pope Francis's reformation to the term "revolutionary." But perhaps, by way of etymology, we might reconcile the realities of his apostolic actions grounded so deeply as they are in tradition and the popular perception of a new wind blowing through the church when he was elected to the Holy See. Going to the root of the Latin term "revolution," we discover *revolutio*, that is, "a turning back, a return." To be a revolutionary means, thus, to accomplish a new action, bring it to a conclusion without leaving one's orbit, without missing the point of return. Pope Francis's reforming impulse has a center of gravity well situated in the context of history, tradition, and Church teaching, and an impulse toward breadth that seeks to reach out and touch everywhere, no matter how remote, throughout the social cosmos so as to bring this message from the center out to the edges.

The engine of this process, the source of his evangelizing energy, which is—even in an astronomical sense, yes—"revolutionary," is Bergoglio's declaration of his own sense of sinfulness: "The finger Jesus points like this . . . toward Matthew. That's me. That's how I feel. Like Matthew. . . . Yes, that's me, 'a sinner toward whom Jesus turns his eyes.'"[8] With these words, Bergoglio describes himself as a disciple of Christ, whose deep conversion came from feeling God's mercy in his own life, and therein lies his strength. This is where is made explicit his purpose in being effective, by way of what he says and how he says it, with the aim of establishing in modern society a level of horizontal communication, which is the only way to create a dialogue between believer and nonbeliever, those who have lost their way on the path of faith or those who have gotten distracted from following the word of Jesus; because in the last analysis, what matters is that every individual faces with his or her own conscience the universal problem of good versus evil.

Pope Francis further says that

> a proclamation in the missionary style concentrates on what is essential, on what is necessary, which is also that which instills passion and is the most attractive, that which makes the heart burn, as with the disciples on the road to Emmaus. We therefore have to find a new balance, otherwise the moral structure of the Church risks falling down like a house of cards, losing the freshness and fragrance of the Gospel. Proclamation of the Gospel must be simple, profound, dazzling. It is from this that then come afterward questions of morality.[9]

In fact, "every time the Church says 'no,' it does so on the basis of a higher and more compelling 'yes': yes to the dignity and value of every human life, which the Church affirms because it has embraced Jesus as Lord and proclaims him to a world increasingly tempted to measure human beings by their utility rather than their dignity," claims George Weigel, with reference to what he terms "Francis's radical Christocentrism."[10]

Starting from these deep roots in the Gospel, Bergoglio has built for himself a certain popularity from knowing how to speak to contemporary people without fear of hearing about realities with which he is unfamiliar, and indeed, on the contrary, recognizing the values of such realities. His revolutionary travels have brought him among peoples, cultures, and values such that the Gospel Word is not simply an act of communication but becomes the communication itself. Bergoglio is following a path set in place nearly a half century before with the Second Ecumenical Vatican Council, and it is no coincidence that the Extraordinary Jubilee of Mercy opened on the same day as the fiftieth anniversary of the closing of Vatican II—December 8, 1965 to 2015, tracing out thereby a path of continuity. His revolution, that is to say, his return, is indeed to this Council, following ideals that link him to John XXIII and Paul VI. But we need not overlook his own way of acting, his determination to redirect the attention of the Church and the world toward Jesus Christ, the continuity he also shares with his two immediate predecessors, John Paul II and Benedict XVI. Indeed, continuity in change.

Piece by piece, from his homilies to his public meetings, from his encyclicals through his apostolic visits, what has taken shape is a comprehensive work of communication that, despite its apparent simplicity, has a certain subtlety to it: "We could say that simplicity and complexity jointly preside over Pope Francis's way of thinking. Simplicity and immediacy in transmitting an *idea*, warmth and strength in communicating a *feeling*, harmony and complexity in offer an *image*."[11]

In his way, Pope Francis's communicative action activates an "interconnectedness based on a rediscovered embrace between humanity and Gospel."[12] And as he himself writes in *Evangelii gaudium*,

> Goodness always tends to spread. Every authentic experience of truth and goodness seeks by its very nature to grow within us, and any person who has experienced a profound liberation becomes more sensitive to the needs of others. As it expands, goodness takes root and develops.[13]

NOTES

Introduction

1. Statement on the awarding of the international journalism prize Argil: European Man to Pope Francis as a "global communicator," European Commission in Italy, December 13, 2013.

2. H. Chua-Eoan and E. Dias, "Pope Francis, the People's Pope," *Time*, December 11, 2013.

3. N. Gibbs, "Pope Francis, the Choice," *Time*, December 11, 2013.

4. Cf. A. J. Greimas, *Du sens: Essais sémiotiques* (Paris: Seuil, 1970).

5. Francis, message for the 48th World Communication Day, "Communication at the Service of an Authentic Culture of Encounter," June 1, 2014. All citations from Pope Francis, including all these quoted here, are available on the Vatican website, https://w2.vatican.va.

6. R. Barthes, *Le degré zéro de l'écriture, suivi de noueavux essais critiques* (Paris: Seuil, 1953).

One: Francis: Plain and Simple

1. Francis, press conference on the return flight from his apostolic journey to Rio de Janeiro, Brazil, on the occasion of the 28th World Youth Day, July 28, 2013.

2. Here are some excerpts from the first address of the newly elected Pope John Paul II, given the evening of October 16, 1978: "Dearest brothers and sisters . . . the most eminent cardinals have called a new Bishop of Rome. They have called

him from a faraway land. . . . I don't know if I can make myself clear in your . . . our Italian language. If I make mistakes, you will correct me."

3. Cf. G. Mazza, ed., *Karol Woytiła, un pontefice in diretta: Sfida e incanto nel rapporto tra Giovanni Paolo II e la TV*, collected papers of the conference, *Evento religioso, evento televisivo, Giovanni Paolo II* (Rome: Pontifical Gregorian University, April 6–7, 2006); D. E. Viganò, *La Chiesa nel tempo dei media* (Rome: Edizioni OCD, 2008).

4. A. Grasso, "Quel silenzio in mezzo del discorso," in *Corriere della Sera*, March 14, 2013.

5. D. Dayan and E. Katz, *Media Events: The Live Broadcasting of History* (Cambridge, MA: Harvard University Press, 1994), 160–61. The basic notion, in reality, is not from Dayan and Katz but is drawn from the conceptual notion of the liminal-liminoid, a legacy of the cultural anthropology studies of Victor W. Turner and A. van Gennep. Of the former, we note *From Ritual to Theatre: The Human Seriousness of Play* (New York: Performing Arts Journal Publications, 1982); *The Ritual Process: Structure and Anti-Structure* (Chicago: Aldine, 1969); *Are There Universals of Performance in Myth, Ritual and Drama?* in R. Schechner, and W. Appel, eds., *By Means of Performance: Intercultural Studies of Theatre and Ritual* (Cambridge: Cambridge University Press, 1990), 8–18.

6. Cf. D. E. Viganò, *Fedeltà è cambiamento: La svolta di Francesco raccontato da vicino* (Rome: RAI ERI, 2015). Idem, "La comunicazione del contatto," in *Cosmopolis* 10, no. 1 (2014), an online journal published by the Department of Philosophy, Linguistics and Literature, Università degli Studi, Perugia.

7. Dayan and Katz, *Media Events*, 195. This attention given to the utopian (or optative) "subjunctive" is likewise a legacy of

the anthropological studies concerning the concept of the limi-noid. Cf. G. Mazza, "Liminalità, comunicazione, coesistenza: transazioni nomadiche dell'identità socio-tecnologica," *Ricerche Teologiche* 17, no. 2 (2006): 427–53.

8. J. Bergoglio, *Papa Francesco. Il nuovo Papa si racconta: Conversazione con Sergio Rubin e Francesca Ambrogetti* (Milan: Salani, 2013).

9. Francis, general audience, *The Family—2. The Mother,* January 7, 2015.

10. Francis, "Storia di una vocazione," *L'Osservatore Romano,* December 23–24, 2013.

11. It is actually from a homily by St. Bede the Venerable, commenting on the Gospel story of the call of St. Matthew, from which the words of this motto are taken: *"Vidit ergo Iesus publicanum et quia miserando atque eligendo vidit, ait illi, Sequere me"* ("A publican saw Jesus and as he looked upon him with a feeling of love and chose him, he said to him, 'Follow me'"), Homily 21, Corpus Christianorum Latinorum (CCL), (Turnhout: Brepols, 1955), 122:149–51.

12. Interview with Pope Francis, "Il tempo della misericor-dia è ora," in A. Rizzzolo, ed., *Credere,* December 6, 2015, 6–14.

13. Perhaps another example of that fertile silence that lis-tens and which Bergoglio will remain faithful to—as we have already seen—right from the start of his first public appearance, after his election to the Chair of St. Peter. In the paradigm set forth concerning his philosophy of language, in listening to the world and to others, and in his understanding of himself and of others, we perceive the dual silences of openness (availability) and closure (because in speaking there must always be a corre-sponding silence). See A. Jacob, *Introduction à la philosophie du langage* (Paris: Gallimard, 1976).

14. Francis, "Storia di una vocazione."

15. Ibid.

16. M. Revuelta González, *Once calas en la Historia de la Compañía de Jesús: "Servir a todo en el Señor"* (Madrid: Universidad Pontificia de Comillas, 2006), 116.

17. Francis, morning meditation in the chapel of the Domus Sanctae Marthae, May 8, 2013.

18. Cf. Francis, homily for the Ordinary Public Consistory for the Creation of New Cardinals, February 22, 2014; *Evangelii gaudium*, November 23, 2013.

19. A. Tornielli, "Carrierismo e vanità, peccati nella Chiesa," in *La Stampa—Vatican Insider*, March 14, 2012.

20. Francis, Address at the Presentation of Christmas Greeting to the Roman Curia, December 22, 2014.

21. Pope Francis will return to this issue again in meeting with students, in a response to one of their questions: "Well, I believe it is not only a matter of wealth. For me it is a question of personality: that is what it is. I need to live with people, and were I to live alone, perhaps a little isolated, it wouldn't be good for me. I was asked this question by a teacher: 'But why don't you go and live there?' I replied: 'Please listen, professor, it is for psychological reasons.' It is my personality. Also, the apartments [in the Papal Palace] are not so luxurious, they are peaceful ... however, I cannot live alone, do you understand? And then I believe, yes; the times speak to us of such great poverty throughout the world, and this is a scandal. The poverty of the world is a scandal. In a world where there is such great wealth, so many resources for giving food to everyone, it is impossible to understand how there could be so many hungry children, so many children without education, so many poor people! Poverty today cries out. We must all think about whether we can become a little poorer. This is something we must all do. How

I can become a little poorer to be more like Jesus, who was the poor teacher. This is the thing. But it is not a problem of my personal virtue; it is only that I cannot live alone, and the matter of the car, as you said: to not have too many things and to become a little poorer. It is this." Address to the students of the Jesuit schools of Italy and Albania, June 7, 2013.

22. Interview with Pope Francis, by J. Berretta, "La gente me hace bien," in *La Voz del Pueblo*, May 24, 2015 (published under the title "Mi manca il camminare per le strade," in *L'Osservatore Romano*, May 25–26, 2015). Cf. J. M. Bergoglio, *Risponde papa Francesco: Tutte le interviste e le conferenze stampa* (Venice: Marsilio, 2015), 281–90.

23. That simplicity of expression has a teaching function is also demonstrated by the language used in advertising, which rediscovered how effective it is quite some time ago, even while navigating the complexity of cultural coding: see G. Gadotti, "La 'semplicità' nella comunicazione pubblicitaria," in *Aperture* 8 (2000): 53–58; D. E. Viganò, *Chiesa e pubblicità: Storia e analisi degli spot 8x1000* (Soveria Mannelli [CZ]: Rubbettino, 2012).

24. Pope Francis's first publication is the encyclical *Lumen fidei*, on June 29, 2013, cowritten with his predecessor, Pope Benedict XVI.

25. Francis, audience with the representatives of the media, March 16, 2013.

26. V. M. Fernández and P. Rodari, *Il progetto di Francesco: Dove vuole portare la Chiesa* (Bologna: EMI, 2014), 21.

27. Vatican Television Center interview with Dario Fo, in the production of the documentary *27 Aprile 2014—Racconto di un evento*, in collaboration with Sky3D and screened at the 9th Festival internazionale del film di Roma (now Festa del cinema di Roma).

28. Ibid.

29. Cf. E. Goffman, *Behavior in Public Places: Notes on the Social Organizations of Gatherings* (New York: Free Press of Glencoe, 1963); E. Goffman, *Interaction Ritual: Essays in Face-to-Face Behavior* (Chicago: Aldine, 1967).

30. Benedict XVI, Message for the 46th World Communications Day, *Silence and Word: Path of Evangelization*, January 24, 2012.

31. St. Augustine, *Commento al Vangelo di San Giovanni* (Rome: Città Nuova, 1968), 405.

32. Cf. P. Watzlawick, J. H. Beavin, and D. D. Jackson, *Pragmatics of Human Communication: A Study of Interactional Patterns, Pathologies, and Paradoxes* (New York: Norton, 1967).

33. M. Accorinti, "Sociologia della comunicazione," in D. E. Viganò, ed., *Dizionario della comunicazione* (Rome: Carocci, 2009), 581–97, quoted from pp. 582–83.

34. Cf. R. Barthes, *Eléments de sémiologie* (Paris: Seuil, 1964).

35. Ibid., viii.

36. Thomas of Celano, *Vita seconda di San Francesco d'Assisi* in *Fonti Francescani*, 681. Paolo Valesio's beautiful reflections on silence as a fullness that touches upon *poesis* come to mind here and, in a semiological key, make clear its most effective metalinguistic function: see P. Valesio, *Ascoltare in silenzio: La retorica come teoria* (Bologna: il Mulino, 1986); cf. G. P. Caprettini, *Principi di semiologia* (Turin: Giappichelli, 1978), 161–79.

37. Francis, general audience, *The Church—6. Catholic and Apostolic*, September 17, 2014, no. 2.

38. *Laudato si'*, May 24, 2015, no. 11.

39. Ibid., no. 16.

40. Ibid., no. 3.

41. R. Barthes, *Le degré zéro de l'écriture, suivi de noueavux essais critiques* (Paris: Seuil, 1953).

42. The reference is obviously to the well-known W. J. Ong, *Orality and Literacy: The Technologizing of the Word* (London and New York: Methuen, 1982).

43. A. Spadaro, "Introduzione," in J. M Bergoglio/Pope Francis, *Nel cuore di ogni padre: Alle radici della mia spiritualità* (Milan: Rizzoli, 2014), 6–23, quoted from p. 9.

44. Cf. Z. Bauman, *Liquid Life* (Cambridge: Polity, 2005). Cf. also Z. Bauman, *Futuro liquido: Società, uomo, politica e filosofia* (Milan: AlboVersorio, 2014); Z. Bauman and C. Bordoni, *State of Crisis* (Cambridge: Polity, 2014).

45. Francis, morning meditation in the chapel of the Domus Sanctae Marthae, September 5, 2014 (revised in *L'Osservatore Romano*, September 6, 2014).

46. Ignatius of Loyola, *Esercizi spirituali*, rule 314 (cf., for example, the San Paolo edition, Milan: Cinisello, Balsamo, 2014).

47. Francis, address to the Renewal in the Holy Spirit Movement, July 3, 2015.

48. Ibid.

49. Francis, morning meditation in the chapel of the Domus Sanctae Marthae, April 24, 2015 (published in *L'Osservatore Romano*, April 25, 2015). The "grace of memory" had already been invoked by Pope Bergoglio in the morning meditation of October 7, 2014. On that occasion as well, the pontiff invited those listening not to forget the story of his own election, along the lines of St. Paul. There he said: "The call to remember arises from the realization that this approach is not a very common tendency among us. We forget things, we live in the moment, and then we forget the history. However, each of us has a history: a history of grace, a history of sin, a history of the journey. This is why it's good to pray with our history . . . to remember

the choice that God made about us; to remember our covenant journey. This means asking oneself whether this covenant has been respected or not. And because fundamentally we are sinners, to pray means first of all to remember the promise that God makes to us and that he never betrays this promise, that is our hope, this is the true prayer" ("Lest We Forget," published with revisions in *L'Osservatore Romano*, October 8, 2014).

50. Interview with Pope Francis by Antonio Spadaro, in *La civiltà cattolica* 3918 (September 19, 2013): 449–77, quoted from p. 453.

51. Ibid., 454.

52. W. von Humboldt, *Scritti sul linguaggio 1795–1827* (Naples: Guida, 1989), 200.

53. Cf. D. E. Viganò, *Il brusio del pettegolo: Forme del discredito nella società e nella Chiesa* (Bologna: Dehoniane-EDB, 2016); D. E. Viganò, "La Chiesa e le pratiche di comunicazione virale. Scenari e processi," *Vivens Homo* 26 (January–June 2015): 7–26.

54. Cf. the concept of communicative residue in C. E. Shannon, "A Mathematical Theory of Communication," *Bell Systems Technical Journal* 27 (1948): 379–423, 623–56.

55. Cf. R. Jakobson, *Essais de linguistique générale* (Paris: Éditions de Minuit, 1963).

56. Cf. U. Eco, *Opera aperta: Forma e indeterminazione nelle poetiche contemporanee* (Milan: Bompiani, 2000; 1st ed., 1962); U. Eco, *Trattato di semiotica generale* (Milan: Bompiani, 1975); U. Eco, *Lector in fabula: La cooperazione interpretativa nei testi narrativi* (Milan: Bompiani, 2000; 1st ed., 1979).

57. This subject merits a far more detailed discussion than is possible here. Let us keep in mind how much the development of cultural and media studies, starting with the attention they

began to get in the 1980s and 1990s, contributed to a meaningful deepening of the themes of reception theory. To cite just two worthy studies in this area, see R. Holub, ed., *Teoria della ricezione* (Turin: Einaudi, 1989), and M. Wolf, *Gli effetti sociali dei media* (Milan: Bompiani, 1992).

58. Ignatius of Loyola, *Spiritual Exercises*, rule 326.

59. Francis, address to the pilgrimage from El Salvador, October 30, 2014.

60. Francis, morning meditation in the chapel of the Domus Sanctae Marthae, September 2, 2013 (reported in *L'Osservatore Romano*, September 2–3, 2014).

61. Ibid.

62. Ibid.

63. In some cases it is the same semiotic model of reference that determines this constitutive ambiguity. One can see this, for example, in the short circuit implied in the concept *unlimited semiosis*, according to which meaning "is, in its primary accession, the translation of a sign into another system of signs," so that "the meaning of a sign is the sign into which it must be translated" in an infinitely recursive dynamic of reference (C. S. Peirce, *Collected Papers*, ed. C. Hartshorne, P. Weiss, and A. W. Burks (Cambridge: Belknap, 1931–1966), 4:127, 132 (author's translation); cf. also the stringent conclusion of U. Eco in *The Role of the Reader: Explorations in the Semiotics of Texts* (Bloomington, IN: Indiana University Press, 1995), 198 (author's translation): "This continuous circularity is the normal condition of signification, and even permits communicative processes to use signs to indicate things and states of the world."

64. U. Volli, "Piacere e forme della maldicenza," in M. Livolsi and U. Volli, eds., *Rumor e pettegolezzi: L'importanza della comunicazione informale* (Milan: FrancoAngeli, 2005), 27–38, quoted from p. 34.

65. Ibid., 28.

66. J. L. Austin, *How to Do Things with Words: The William James Lectures Delivered at Harvard University in 1995* (Oxford: Clarendon, 1962).

67. J. L. Austin, *Philosophical Papers* (Oxford: Clarendon, 1961), 129–30.

68. "False notizie," in *L'Osservatore Romano*, October 22, 2015.

69. Francis, morning meditation in the chapel of the Domus Sanctae Marthae, September 2, 2013.

70. "Onze vriend in Rome," in *Straatnieuws* 16, November 6–26, 2015.

71. Francis, morning meditation in the chapel of the Domus Sanctae Marthae, February 3, 2015 (revised by *L'Osservatore Romano*, February 4, 2013).

72. Ibid.

Two: Language and Communication

1. Francis, press conference on the return flight from the visit to the United States, September 27, 2015.

2. P. Ricoeur, *Time and Narrative, Volume 1,* trans. Kathleen McLaughlin and David Pellauer (Chicago and London: University of Chicago Press, 1984), 3.

3. Ibid., translated here from the Italian; original French text unavailable.

4. Ibid., translated here from Italian; original French text unavailable.

5. M. Foucault, *Les mots et les choses: Une archéologie des sciences humaines* (Paris: Gallimard, 1966), translated here from Italian; original French text unavailable.

6. W. J. Ong, *Orality and Literacy: The Technologizing of the Word* (London and New York: Methuen, 1982), 7.

7. E. Cassirer, *Philosophie del symbolischen Formen, vol. 1: Die Sprache* (Berlin: B. Cassirer, 1923).

8. Francis, pastoral visit to Turin, meeting with children and young people, June 21, 2015.

9. Francis, morning meditation in the chapel of the Domus Sanctae Marthae, September 2, 2013.

10. Francis, address to the participants in Rome's Diocesan Conference, June 14, 2015.

11. Francis, address to the 2nd World Meeting of Popular Movements (Expo Feria Exhibition Centre, Santa Cruz de la Sierra, Bolivia), July 9, 2015.

12. M. Baldini, "Storia della comunicazione," in D. E. Viganò, ed., *Dizionario della comunicazione* (Rome: Carocci, 2009), 21–37, quoted from p. 37.

13. I. Calvino, *Lezione americane: Sei proposte per il prossimo millennio* (Milan: Mondadori, 2012; 1st ed., 1988), 60.

14. It is probably true that the matrix of a certain *logocentric approach* to human beings and their knowledge is esconced in that *violent "domination" of the concept* that has distinguished the soul of modern philosophy, starting with Hegel up to recent attempts at "metaphysical hybridization" of the Johannine *logos* (itself an object of irreverent conflation). See the interesting and worthy contribution of M. Ravera and P. D. Bubbio, "'Raccoglier' e 'accogliere.' Riflessioni sul Logos alla luce della critica di Girard a Heidegger," *Filosofia e Teologia* 20 (2006): 472–84. On the relationship between the two *logoi*, see also G. Segalla, "Il Logos eracliteo e il Logos giovanneo. Un dialogo culturale tra i primi lettori dei due testi," *Filosofia e Teologia* 13 (1999): 73–83. On naming and imagery, see G. Mazza, "Immagini del

Nome: uni-pluralità, pseudonimia e trans-figurazioni del Logos incarnato," *Ricerche Teologiche* 19 (2008): 79–94.

15. Francis, *Evangelii gaudium*, November 24, 2013.

16. Francis, *Laudato si'*, May 24, 2015.

17. Francis, *Evangelii gaudium*, November 24, 2013.

18. J. L. Austin, *How to Do Things with Words: The William James Lectures Delivered at Harvard University in 1995* (Oxford: Clarendon, 1962).

19. M. Buber, *Die Schriften über das dialogische Prinzip* (Heidelberg: Lambert Schneider, 1954).

20. Ibid.

21. M. Benasayag and G. Schmit, *Les passions tristes: Souffrance psychique et crise sociale* (Paris: Éditions la Découverte, 2003).

22. D. E. Viganò, *Fedeltà è cambiamento: La svolta di Francesco raccontato da vicino* (Rome: RAI ERI, 2015).

23. Cf. C. Penati, "'Quasi alla fine del mondo.' I primi mesi del pontificato di Francesco nelle immagini del Centra Televisivo Vaticano," in D. E. Viganò, ed., *Telecamere su San Pietro: I trent'anni del Centro Televisivo Vaticano* (Milan: Vita e Pensiero, 2013), 123–29.

24. Analogy is one, for example, "because the resemblances used by it are not the visible, massive ones of the things themselves; it's enough that they consist of the most subtle of relationships. . . . The space of analogies is, fundamentally, a space that radiates. From all around, man is placed in reference to himself; but this same man, in turn, transmits resemblances that are received by the world. It is the great fire of proportions; the center in which relationships converge and find support, and from which they are reflected anew" (M. Foucault, *Les mots et les choses*, translated here from Italian; original French text unavailable).

25. Cf. C. S. Peirce and W. James, *Che cos'è il pragmatismo* (Milan: Jaca Book, 2000). Cf. also in Peirce as in Eco the concept of unlimited semiosis, mentioned in the previous chapter, n. 63.

26. Francis, homily for the Chrism Mass, March 28, 2013.

27. Francis, Vigil of Pentecost with the Ecclesial Movements, May 18, 2013.

28. "I see quite clearly . . . that the thing the Church needs the most is the capacity to heal wounds and to warm the hearts of the faithful, neighborliness, closeness. I see the Church like a field hospital after a battle. It is useless to ask someone who is gravely wounded whether their cholesterol and blood sugar are high! Their wounds must be healed. Then, we can talk about everything else. Heal the wounds, heal the wounds. . . . And we have to start on the ground level" (interview with Pope Francis by Antonio Spadaro, in *La civiltà cattolica* 3918 [September 19, 2013]: 449–77, quoted from pp. 461–62).

29. Francis, address to the parish priests of the Diocese of Rome, March 6, 2014.

30. J. M. Bergoglio/Pope Francis, *Aprite la mente al vostro cuore* (Milan: Rizzoli, 2013), 13.

31. Francis, Vigil of Pentecost with the Ecclesial Movements, May 18, 2013.

32. V. Gigante, "Bergoglio lava più bianco. La rivoluzione a parole di papa Francesco," *Micromega*, July 24, 2013. http://temi.repubblica.it/micromega-online/la-rivoluzione-a-parole-di-papa-francesco/.

33. Francis, address to the bishops of the episcopal conference of Portugal on their "ad limina" visit, September 7, 2015.

34. Francis, interviewed by Aura Vistas Miguel on Rádio Renascença, September 14, 2015; A. V. Miguel, "Entrevista ao

Papa. 'Tenho confiança nos políticos jovens. Há um problema mundial que é a corrupçao.'"

35. Ibid., 4.

36. G. Lakoff and M. Johnson, *Metaphors We Live By* (Chicago: University of Chicago Press, 1980).

37. Proximity and metaphor go hand in hand: crucial metaphors are "those whose interpretation requires a meaningful capacity for intimacy such as to allow the recognition of what is derived from deep personal experience" (G. Corradi Fiumara, *Il processo metaforico: Connessioni tra vita e linguaggio* [Bologna: il Mulino, 1998], 202).

38. http://www.luigiaccattoli.it/blog/conferenze-e-dibattiti-2/la-chiesa-e-la-comunicazione-al-tempo-di-papa-francesco/

39. Francis, address to the participants in the Fifth Convention of the Italian Church, November 10, 2015.

40. Francis, address at the meeting of the bishops of Brazil, during his apostolic visit to Rio de Janeiro on the occasion of the XXVIII World Youth Day, July 27, 2013.

41. Francis, *Evangelii gaudium*, November 23, 2013.

42. Cf. R. Jakobson, *Essais de linguistique générale* (Paris: Éditions de Minuit, 1963). The idea of a physical substrate in the channeling of communicative processes has, however, been the subject of review in the past few years. What has brought discussion of it to the fore is primarily a certain style of virtual experience that has broadened the communicative act beyond its functional mechanics. On this point see all of Lévy's work, and in particular P. Lévy, *Qu'est-ce que le virtuel?* (Paris: La Découverte, 1995).

43. D. E. Viganò, *Fedeltà è cambiamento*.

44. Francis, message for the 49th World Communications Day, January 23, 2015.

45. Ibid.

46. As Benedict XVI likewise mentioned, addressing the theme of digital media: "Woe to me if I do not preach the Gospel" (1 Cor 9:16). The increased availability of the new technologies demands greater responsibility on the part of those called to proclaim the Word, but it also requires them to become more focused, efficient, and compelling in their efforts. Priests stand at the threshold of a new era: as new technologies create deeper forms of relationship across greater distances, they are called to respond pastorally by putting the media ever more effectively at the service of the Word" (Benedict XVI, message for the 44th World Communications Day, "The Priest and Pastoral Ministry in a Digital World: New Media at the Service of the Word," January 24, 2010).

47. E. Cassirer, *Philosophie del symbolischen Formen, vol. 1: Die Sprache* (Berlin: B. Cassirer, 1923), 143 of the Italian translation.

48. Francis, press conference during his flight to the Philippines, January 15, 2015.

49. Meeting with Luigi Accattoli, Università Raimondo Lullo, February 14, 2015. "La Chiesa e la comunicazione al tempo di Papa Francesco." http://www.luigiaccattoli.it/blog/conferenze-e-dibattiti-2/la-chiesa-e-la-comunicazione-al-tempo-di-papa-francesco/.

50. Ibid.

51. Ibid.

52. A. Spadaro, "Le omelie di Santa Marta," in J. M. Bergoglio, *La verità è un incontro: Omelie di Santa Marta* (Milan: Rizzoli, 2014), 11–45, quoted from pp. 23–24.

53. Francis, morning meditation in the chapel of the Domus Sanctae Marthae, January 11, 2014 (reported in *L'Osservatore Romano*, January 12, 2014).

54. Ibid.

55. Ibid.

56. B. Malinowski, *Argonauts of the Western Pacific: An Account of Native Enterprise and Adventure in the Archipelagoes of Melanesian New Guinea* (London: G. Routledge & Sons, 1922).

57. M. Mauss, "Essai sur le don. Forme et raison de l'échange dans les sociétés archaïques," *L'Année sociologique*, second series, 1923–1924.

58. Mauss focuses on what we might define as an economist conception of gift, postulating that it has three necessary components: giving, receiving, and reciprocation. He therefore understands gift primarily as reciprocity and debt: gift because I am indebted and in giving I perpetuate the indebtedness. Subsequent thinkers would argue strongly against this conception, first and foremost Jacques Derrida (*Donner le temps: La fausse monnaie* [Paris: Galilée, 1991]).

59. Francis, Angelus, November 17, 2013.

60. Francis, Angelus, April 6, 2014.

61. Francis, Angelus, February 22, 2015.

62. Francis, Vigil of Pentecost with the Ecclesial Movements, May 18, 2013.

63. Francis, homily at the Chrism Mass, March 28, 2015.

64. Ibid.

65. Ibid.

66. Francis, conversation with journalists during the return flight from Asunción to Rome, apostolic visit to Ecuador, Bolivia, and Paraguay, July 13, 2015.

67. Benedict XVI, message for the 44th World Communications Day, January 24, 2010.

68. Cf. D. E. Viganò, "Il Centro Televisivo Vaticano, il Papa

e la Chiesa in Ultra HD e 3D," in *Apocalittici e integrati 50 anni dopo: Dove va la televisione,* Quaderni di Confindustria Radio Televisioni 1 (Soveria Mannelli [CZ]: Rubbettino, 2015), 104–18.

69. Francis, message for the 48th World Communications Day, "Communication in Service of an Authentic Culture of Encounter," January 24, 2014.

70. A. Fabris, *Etica della comunicazione* (Rome: Carocci, 2006), 81.

71. Cf. P. Peverini, *Social Guerilla: Semiotica della comunicazione non convenzionale* (Rome: Luiss University Press, 2014).

72. Francis, message for the 48th World Communications Day, "Communication in Service of an Authentic Culture of Encounter," January 24, 2014.

73. Ibid.

Three: Encyclicals and Travels

1. Francis, address to the participants in Rome's diocesan conference, June 17, 2015.

2. M. Foucault, *Les mots et les choses: Une archéologie des sciences humaines* (Paris: Gallimard, 1966), translated here from Italian; original French unavailable.

3. J.-F. Lyotard, *La condition postmoderne: Rapport sur le savoir* (Paris: Les Éditions de Minuit, 1979).

4. Francis, interviewed by Aura Vistas Miguel on Rádio Renascença, September 14, 2015; A. V. Miguel, "Entrevista ao Papa. 'Tenho confiança nos políticos jovens. Há um problema mundial que é a corrupçao.'"

5. Francis, address on the South Lawn of the White House, September 23, 2015.

6. Ibid.

7. Francis, address to the Joint Session of the United States Congress, September 24, 2015.

8. Francis, morning meditation in the chapel of the Domus Sanctae Marthae, November 19, 2015 (as reported in *L'Osservatore Romano*, November 20, 2013).

9. M. Figueroa, "Radicato nel Vangelo. Per comprendere Papa Bergoglio," in *L'Osservatore Romano*, November 5, 2015.

10. Francis, Invocation for Peace, Vatican Gardens, June 8, 2014.

11. Francis, homily at Holy Mass during pastoral visit to Assisi, October 4, 2013.

12. Ibid.

13. Francis, *Laudato si'*, May 24, 2015, no. 14.

14. C. Petrini, "Guida alla lettura," in Pope Francis, *Laudato si': Enciclica sulla cura della casa comune* (Cinisello Balsamo [Milan]: Edizioni San Paolo, 2015), 5–23, quoted from pp. 5, 8.

15. Editorial, "The Guardian View on *Laudato Si'*: Pope Francis Calls for a Cultural Revolution," *The Guardian*, June 18, 2015.

16. Francis, *Laudato si'*, May 24, 2015, nos. 12, 14.

17. Ibid., nos. 19, 13, 58, 205.

18. E. Bianchi, "Il Vangelo della creazione," *Vita Pastorale* 8 (August 2015): 18–19.

19. Francis, *Laudato si'*, May 24, 2015, nos. 12, 14.

20. Ibid., no. 18.

21. L. Alici, "Natura e persona: lo *sguardo diverso* di Papa Francesco," in G. Notarstefano, ed., *Abiterai la terra: Commento all'enciclica Laudato si'* (Rome: AVE, 2015), 51–58, quoted from pp. 53–54.

22. L. Goodstein and J. Gillis, "On a Planet in Distress, a Papal Call to Action," *New York Times*, June 18, 2015.

23. Francis, *Laudato si'*, May 24, 2015, no. 16.

24. Francis, *Evangelii gaudium*, November 23, 2013, no. 265.

25. Benedict XVI, *Deus caritas est*, December 25, 2005, no. 1.

26. Francis, morning meditation in the chapel of the Domus Sanctae Marthae, June 15, 2013.

27. Ibid.

28. Francis, homily at the Holy Mass for the closing of the 14th Ordinary General Assembly of the Synod of Bishops, October 25, 2015.

29. J. M. Bergoglio, address to the pre-conclave General Congregations, March 9, 2013, as reported in G. Cardinale, "La Chiesa guardi alle periferie," *Avvenire*, March 27, 2013, p. 3.

30. Miguel, "Entrevista ao Papa," 4–5.

31. Francis, *Evangelii gaudium*, November 23, 2013, no. 20.

32. Ibid., no. 21.

33. M. Gronchi and R. Repole, *Il* dolce stil novo *di papa Francesco* (Padua: Edizioni Messagero Padova, 2015), 32.

34. Francis, morning meditation in the chapel of the Domus Sanctae Marthae, February 5, 2013.

35. Ibid.

36. Francis, *Evangelii gaudium*, November 23, 2013, no. 129.

37. M. I. Rupnik, "Premessa," in G. Busca, *La riconciliazione "sorella del battesimo"* (Rome: Lipa, 2011), 9–10, quoted from p. 9.

38. Pastoral Constitution on the Church in the Modern World, *Gaudium et spes*, December 7, 1965, no. 1.

39. Francis, *Evangelii gaudium*, November 23, 2013, no. 1.

40. V. E. Fernández and P. Rodari, *Il progetto di Francesco: Dove vuole portare la Chiesa* (Bologna: EMI, 2014), 23.

41. "Furthering the teaching of *Evangelii nuntiandi* of Paul VI, he once again puts at the center the person of Jesus Christ,

the first evangelizer, who calls each of us today to participate with him in the work of salvation" (12). "Missionary activity is the paradigm for every work of the Church" (15)—states the Holy Father—which necessitates taking the time to discern and live out a "new stage" in evangelization (17) (R. Fisichella, press conference for the presentation of apostolic exhortation *Evangelii gaudium* by the Holy Father on the proclamation of the Gospel to the modern world, November 23, 2013).

42. Ignatius of Loyola, *Spiritual Exercises*, rule 336.

43. Francis, *Evangelii gaudium*, November 23, 2013, no. 15.

44. Ibid., no. 11.

45. Ibid., no. 32.

46. Fernández and Rodari, *Il progetto di Francesco*, 34.

47. M. Foucault, *Les mots et les choses: Une archéologie des sciences humaines* (Paris: Gallimard, 1966), translated here from Italian; original French text unavailable.

48. G. Marrone, "L'efficacia simbolica dello spazio: azioni e passioni," in P. Berretti and G. Manetti, eds., *Forme della testualità: Teorie, modelli, storia e prospettive*, Acts of the Annual Conference of the Associazione italiana di studi semiotici, *Testi & Immagine* (Turin, 2001), 344–61, quoted from p. 346. It would be interesting to verify the effectiveness with which access to "narrative space" flows into a static concept of space as a volumetric dimension or, metaphorically, as indicative of a *status quo* that is an expression of power, control, or ownership. *Evangelii gaudium* is in this way, too, extremely provocative, urging the start of processes rather than the occupation of spaces (see nos. 222–37). Cf. G. Mazza, "Processare l'evento cristiano: riflessioni a margine di *Evangelii gaudium*," *Annali di Studi Religiosi* 16 (2015): 57–73.

49. M. McCombs and D. Shaw, "The Agenda-Setting Func-

tion of Mass Media," *Public Opinion Quarterly* 36 (1972): 176–87, translated here from Italian; original English text unavailable. Cf. also R. Marini, *Mass media e discussion pubblica: Le teorie dell'agenda setting* (Rome and Bari: Laterza, 2006).

50. Francis, homily, visit to Lampedusa, July 8, 2013.

51. Francis, address during meeting with business people and workers, pastoral visit to Cagliari, September 22, 2013.

52. Ibid.

53. Francis, morning meditation in the chapel of the Domus Sanctae Marthae, May 1, 2013.

54. Francis, address at the prayer vigil with young people, Rio de Janeiro, July 27, 2013.

55. Francis, meeting with journalists during the flight to Rio de Janeiro, July 22, 2013.

56. S. Centofani, *Il viaggio di Papa Francesco a Cuba e negli USA in 10 punti*, September 29, 2015. http://it.radiovaticana.va/news/2015/09/29/il_viaggio_di_papa_francesco_a_cuba_e_negli_usa_in_10_punti/1175512.

57. Ibid.

58. Cf. "The Chosun Ilbo," August 18, 2014. This article reports on the visit to the Kkottongnae House of Hope during which the pope bent his arms in the shape of a heart. Thus, the resemblance to which the newspaper refers.

59. Francis, homily at the Holy Mass of the Solemnity of the Assumption, World Cup Stadium in Daejon, August 15, 2014.

60. Francis, address at the meeting with authorities and diplomatic corps, Bangui, Central African Republic, November 29, 2015.

61. Francis, address at the opening of the Holy Door, Cathedral of Bangui, Central African Republic, November 29, 2015.

62. Ibid.

Notes

Conclusion

1. Francis, homily at the Holy Mass and opening of the Holy Door, St. Peter's Square, December 8, 2015.

2. Francis, Bull of Indiction of the Extraordinary Jubilee of Mercy, *Misericordiae Vultus*, April 11, 2015.

3. Ibid.

4. Francis, homily at the Holy Mass and opening of the Holy Door, St. Peter's Square, December 8, 2015.

5. Francis, Angelus, December 8, 2015.

6. Francis, press conference during the flight from Santiago, Cuba, to Washington, DC, September 22, 2015.

7. S. Falasca, "Quell che avrei detto al consistoro. Intervista con il Cardinale Jorge Mario Bergoglio, Arcivescovo di Buenos Aires," *30 Giorni* 11 (2007): 18–21, quoted from p. 20.

8. Interview with Pope Francis by Antonio Spadaro, in *La civiltà cattolica* 3918 (September 19, 2013): 449–77, quoted from p. 452.

9. Ibid., 464.

10. G. Weigel, "The Christ-Centered Pope: The Catholic Church and the World Wrestle with an Evangelical Papacy," *National Review*, September 20, 2013.

11. M. Gronchi and R. Repole, *Il dolce stil novo di papa Francesco* (Padua: Edizioni Messagero Padova, 2015), 22.

12. D. E. Viganò, "Francesco nel villaggio globale. Lo stile comunicativo di Bergoglio tra oralità e concretezza," *L'Osservatore Romano*, July 16, 2015.

13. Francis, *Evangelii gaudium*, November 23, 2013, no. 9.

About the Author

Dario Edoardo Viganò is an Italian Catholic priest, writer, and university teacher. He served as Director of the Vatican Television Center from 2013 to 2018. He participated in the Administrative Council of the Centro Sperimentale di Cinematografia with responsibilities covering the Italian National Film Archives and publishing. Since 2005 he has been a lecturer in Semiology of Cinema and Audiovisual Technology and Cinema Theory and Techniques in the faculty of Political Science and Communication Studies at the LUISS Guido Carli University in Rome. He was made a member of the Pontifical Academy of Theology and of the scientific board of the Centre for Media and Communication Studies (CMCS) "Massimo Baldini." He is also a member of the scientific board of the CMCS-LUISS Working Papers Series. In 1998, he became a member of the Italian Episcopal Conference.

About the Translator

Robert H. Hopcke is the author of numerous works in the field of Jungian psychology and Roman Catholic spirituality. He has translated a variety of books in fields as diverse as art history, sexuality, and religion, including most recently, with Paul A. Schwartz, *The Little Flowers of St. Francis*, from Shambhala Publications.

About the Publisher

The Crossroad Publishing Company publishes Crossroad and Herder & Herder books. We offer a 200-year global family tradition of books on spiritual living and religious thought. We promote reading as a time-tested discipline for focus and understanding. We help authors shape, clarify, write, and effectively promote their ideas. We select, edit, and distribute books. With our expertise and passion, we provide wholesome spiritual nourishment for heart, mind, and soul through the written word.

Photo Descriptions and Credits

Chapter One

Page 8

Pope Francis Cardinal Jorge Mario Bergoglio was elected Pope on March 13, 2013 by the Conclave.

Chapter Two

Page 56

Pope Francis surrounded by women in white dresses when he arrived on January 10, 2018 at the airport in Trujillo, Peru.

Chapter Three

Page 100

Prisoners lock arms during the welcoming of Pope Francis, to the Prison of Paliano, 60 kilometers southwest of Rome on April 13, 2017. He washed the feet of twelve prisoners from Italy, Argentina, and Albania.